Paul Waddington is the author of *Seasonal Food* and *21st Century Smallholder*. He tries to live as sustainably as possible with his wife and two children.

www.rbooks.co.uk/eden

Also by Paul Waddington

Seasonal Food
21st Century Smallholder

SHADES OF GREEN

A (mostly) practical A–Z for the reluctant
environmentalist

Paul Waddington

eden project books

TRANSWORLD PUBLISHERS
61–63 Uxbridge Road, London W5 5SA
A Random House Group Company
www.rbooks.co.uk

First published in Great Britain
in 2008 by Eden Project Books
an imprint of Transworld Publishers

A CIP catalogue record for this book
is available from the British Library.

ISBN 9781905811007

Addresses for Random House Group Ltd companies outside the UK
can be found at: www.randomhouse.co.uk
The Random House Group Ltd Reg. No. 954009

The Random House Group Ltd supports The Forest Stewardship Council (FSC),
the leading international forest-certification organization. All our titles that are printed
on Greenpeace-approved FSC-certified paper carry the FSC logo.
Our paper procurement policy can be found at
www.rbooks.co.uk/environment

Mixed Sources
Product group from well-managed
forests and other controlled sources
www.fsc.org   Cert no. TT-COC-2139
© 1996 Forest Stewardship Council
FSC

Typeset in 12.25/15 pt Weiss BT by Falcon Oast Graphic Art Ltd.

Printed and bound in Great Britain by
CPI Mackays, Chatham, ME5 8TD

4 6 8 10 9 7 5 3

Introduction

Just exactly how 'green' are the various choices we make? Is it 'better' to use a dishwasher or wash up by hand? Is local food always 'greener' than stuff that has travelled thousands of 'food miles'? Where are hybrid cars on a scale where 1 is tremendously green and 10 is Jeremy Clarkson? Is it better to sign up for green-tariff electricity or to stick a windmill on your roof? It's often difficult to navigate the green minefield. There are a couple of good reasons for this. The main one is that we need to take a common view of what 'green' actually means. Does it always mean low mpg, low food miles, low technology and no fun? Or does it sometimes mean choices that are a bit less obvious? The second complication is that there are plenty of people out there telling us that their solution is the greenest, when maybe it isn't.

'Greenness' used to be about railing against industrial and agricultural pollution, supporting biodiversity, saving the whale, finding alternatives to dwindling oil reserves. It's still about these things – and thanks to the efforts of green campaigners we have cleaner rivers, tighter environmental legislation and a much better awareness of environmental issues. However, if we are to accept the global scientific consensus (and the few who reject it mostly have some sort of ideological axe to grind) then the big deal today is greenhouse gases, in particular CO_2, of which human activity produces more than the biosphere can comfortably deal with. Divide a sustainable level of anthropogenic (human-generated) CO_2 emissions by the world's population and you come to an amount which each of us should emit: this is currently 2.4 tonnes per person per annum, a quarter of the UK's current per-person CO_2 emissions of around 10 tonnes.

So the definition of 'green' in this book is firstly about the degrees to which the choices we make result in CO_2 emissions. Put this into context and it can look dispiriting. Britain is responsible for 2 per cent of global anthropogenic CO_2 emissions. Of these, less than 50 per cent are the domestic emissions we can easily control with our choices; and of these, space- and water-heating, travel and our food choices are the most influential. Feeling morose about it, we could mumble that even if, say, we all changed our light bulbs tomorrow, on a global scale it would affect a fraction of 3 per cent of a fraction of 2 per cent of energy use. It is undeniable that in the global scheme of things, successfully lobbying China to mandate total carbon-capture and storage technology in each new coal-fired power station it allegedly opens every week will have a vastly bigger impact on greenhouse-gas emissions than anything we can do in our houses. But lots of small changes 'scaled up' to national level have had a measurable impact before and are having one now: unleaded petrol, CFC-free aerosols or the move to mandatory energy-efficient boilers.

Beyond CO_2 emissions, 'green' in this book also denotes activities that use resources (e.g. water, agricultural land, wild fish) at a sustainable level, and that have no net deleterious effect on the biosphere. Here, again, small changes can make a big difference nationally, whether it's toilets that use half as much water or detergents that chuck fewer phosphates into our rivers.

But whatever choice it is you are contemplating – and despite what the vendors of wind turbines, hybrid cars or eco-holidays might suggest to you – being green is never black and white. There are always shades in between. And whilst many of us may have decided not to do the least green thing, the very greenest thing may be too extreme.

So what are the 'shades of green' in the choices we make? Using an informal ranking that runs from 'deep green' to 'not even a little bit green', this book identifies and explains them. It's not a rigid, scientific scale with green 'points'; it's designed to give you an idea of how green various different choices are. They are not always what you would expect; nor are they always strictly practical. Nor does the book cover all the choices we make; but for the things that have been omitted, you will most likely be able to work out the 'shades of green' for yourself. The things that have been chosen are those that have the most important environmental effect, and those that have interesting or unexpected 'shades'.

The good news is, that whatever the choice you are making, in most cases there is a shade of green for everyone.

Aeroplanes

'*The best thing we can do with environmentalists is shoot them.*' *Ryanair boss Michael O'Leary's decidedly un-relaxed attitude to green issues, hinted at in this November 2005 quote, shows how touchy the aviation industry can be about its rapidly growing environmental impact. It may account for only around 2–5.5 per cent of the UK's CO_2 emissions (depending on whether you believe the industry or the government), but the issue with aviation overall is its projected rate of growth set against the CO_2 reduction targets to which the UK has committed itself. Emissions from the UK air-transport industry have more than doubled since 1990. Put the government's forecast aviation growth by 2050 next to its commitment to reduce CO_2 emission by 60 per cent by the same year, and aviation will account for half of all CO_2 the country is allowed to emit. Go for the more serious emissions reductions that many are recommending, and no other activities would be allowed to produce any CO_2 if aviation continued to grow at current rates. The twin problems with aviation are the distances involved, which result in very large volumes of greenhouse gas per passenger; and the fact that those emissions, deposited as they are at high altitudes, cause additional 'radiative forcing' effects which are estimated to multiply the effect of the emissions 2.7 times. So even without the forcing effect, a family of four's round trip to Disneyland in Florida puts nearly 8 tonnes of CO_2 into the atmosphere: it would take 48,270 kilometres of driving in the family Mondeo to create the same emissions. With no significant efficiency gains in aircraft coming any time soon, it ain't easy to fly and be green.*

Deep green:
No flying

Relax into an airliner's seat and you will emit less CO_2 per passenger kilometre than if you were in the back of a taxi. The difference, of course, is that despite the often wild claims of their drivers, taxis can't cover the 5,585 kilometres to New York in seven hours and they don't pollute the upper atmosphere. Just two such return flights will blow your entire annual 'sustainable' carbon allowance of 2.4 tonnes per year (see p. 1). Short-haul flights are marginally less of an issue in carbon terms: London to Manchester by car potentially emits more CO_2 than flying – however, that's only if there's one person in the car. But short flights are less fuel-efficient overall because of the large fuel burn in take-off and landing. Even at its relatively economical cruising speed, an Airbus A320 (itself not a particular gas-guzzler amongst airliners) will burn through an average British car's annual fuel consumption in 36 minutes. And the hugely disruptive noise pollution from aviation, the environmental impacts of airports and lower-level atmospheric pollution all conspire with its global-warming impact to make it one of the least green of human activities. There are shades of green with most of the things we do – but not many with flying. If you do fly to any significant degree, stopping flying or flying as little as possible is the single most environmentally positive thing you can do.

Dark green:
No flying (see above)

Quite green:
No flying (see above)

Light green:
No flying (see above)

Pale green:
Extremely infrequent flying, offset, preferably, with serious carbon-reducing lifestyle changes

Many deep greenies blanch at the mere suggestion of flying and have resigned themselves to a future of long, complex train journeys or slow sojourns by sea, local holidays and video-conferencing. But some of us have to fly, some of the time. You can offset your emissions, of course: it costs about twelve quid to offset the New York return flight by contributing to schemes that reduce CO_2 elsewhere. But offsetting is fraught with controversy and riddled with eco-snake-oil salesmen. Will the money that the offsetter invests on your behalf in, say, a developing-world renewable energy project really compensate for the big chunk of greenhouse gas you have just delivered directly into the stratosphere? Does offsetting every flight – even with the most reputable offsetting firm – make it OK to carry on as before? There are no straight answers to these questions: but doing something positive is always better than doing nothing. If you have to fly and wish to 'atone' for it in a way that you can measure yourself, then major carbon-reducing lifestyle changes are the best way forward: tackling car use (see p. 54) and domestic space-and-water

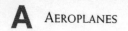

heating (see p. 137) will take the biggest bites out of your carbon footprint.

Not even a little bit green:
Personal airliner

Time was when Concorde was the best way to give the planet a good kicking. Guzzling 13,000 litres of kerosene per hour at full power, and double that when its afterburners were lit up for take-off, Concorde made a small private jet look like an environmental statement. With only one hundred passengers and flying at a high altitude where its emissions could do the maximum damage, Concorde was the eco-hooligan's ride of choice. Today, sadly, with private jets consuming a measly 600 or so litres per hour and Concorde no longer available, planetary vandals must look elsewhere. A private airliner is the best solution: the Boeing 767 purchased by the founders of Google (informal motto: 'Don't be evil') and reportedly fitted out for fifty passengers would, with its 7,400 litres per hour kerosene habit, give a per-person fuel consumption that puts Concorde in the shade and even beats the mighty Air Force One.

MORE INFORMATION
Offsetting flights: www.climatecare.org

Apples

Apples provoke much dithering amongst those who fret about fruit and the environment. And rightly so, for the search for the sustainable apple is fraught with tricky detail. The problem is mainly about climate and its consequences. The season during which fresh British apples can be plucked from trees runs from late July to October. For the other two-thirds of the year, the apples we eat are either stored locally grown varieties or imports, from as far away as New Zealand. Storage, these days, mostly means refrigeration, which needs power. And with the relatively low fuel consumption per apple of sea freight, some antipodean apples may be responsible for fewer overall emissions than British ones that have spent many months in an industrial fridge. Then there is the organic issue: pest- and disease-prone apples are difficult to grow organically on a commercial scale and yields are 25 per cent lower. Yet conventional apples often contain residues of the many substances with which they are sprayed. What is the green apple consumer to do?

Deep green:
Your own apples, traditional storage

This is not as daft as it sounds. Assuming that an average British garden is 100 square metres and a small orchard could be planted on half of it, this could provide an annual yield of 50kg of apples, which adds up to just over an apple a day. Not enough to keep the doctor away for the whole family, but almost enough to meet an average family of four's 64kg per year apple habit. Plant a good range of varieties and you will be able to start with fresh apples in August and then store good 'keepers' like Bramleys through the winter and spring. Storage needs cool, dark, well-ventilated spaces: attics will fit the bill in the cooler months. Apple trees are good-looking, have superb blossom that will be appreciated by any bees you may also be keeping and, as other outdoor activities can go on beneath them, they need not monopolize the garden.

Deep green 2:
Seasonal, local, organic, direct, then traditionally stored

There is a rich but fading heritage of apple-growing in Britain, with thousands of varieties catalogued, in contrast to the few that regularly appear on most supermarket shelves. Thanks to the effects of agricultural policy and globalization, British apple production has declined steeply in recent years, to the extent that since 1970 we have lost two-thirds of our orchards. Britain now imports more than twice as many apples as it produces, mostly from France and then from South Africa and New Zealand, whose southern-hemisphere climates fill the fresh-apple gap. All of this apple trade carries an environmental cost and the best way to minimize it is to buy apples in season from as nearby as possible. Buying organic means that the environmental impact of apple-growing will have been greatly reduced. 'Conventional' (that bizarre term) apples are sprayed 14–18 times a year with 30–38 active substances, including fungicides, insecticides, herbicides and growth regulators. All of which uses plenty of energy and has the not entirely surprising result that 80 per cent of apples recently sampled had detectable pesticide residues. If it is possible to find apples that have been stored in a more traditional manner out of season, perhaps at a farmers' market or direct from a grower, then this will give you the lowest-impact out-of-season apple.

Dark green:
Just seasonal and local

Growing organic apples on a commercial scale is not easy; and the rarity of organic Coxes attests to the fact that this favoured variety is more disease-prone than most. So now comes that great apple-shopping question: is it better to buy the organic ones from afar or the conventional ones from Britain? As with many things green, there is no black-and-white answer. If it's a choice between conventional ones from Britain that come from a modern, intensive orchard (where there is little room for biodiversity) and are sold through a food-miles-intensive super-market, then the overseas organics are probably a better bet. If, however, the British apples are not organic but grown by a smaller-scale producer and sold direct or through a farmers' market or local greengrocer, then they probably have a lower impact than apples that had a lovely hippy start in life but then travelled 11,000 miles in a floating refrigerator.

Light green:
Commercially stored British apples in winter and spring

Now we really are getting into the detail. A long-storing British Bramley hoiked out of the fridge in June may have spent eight months in there, whereas a New Zealand Braeburn that has been harvested in March and shipped straight to the UK will have needed only half the refrigeration. Does the shipping tip the balance in the Bramley's favour? Possibly; but what's certain is that the less time the apple has spent in refrigerated storage, the less fuel will have been expended on it. So in the winter and early spring, when our own season has finished but before the southern-hemisphere one starts, stored British apples, which have not made a long journey in less efficient mobile refrigeration, have the environmental edge.

Pale green:
Southern-hemisphere imports outside the British apple season

There is a study (see also in relation to lamb, p. 154) that shows New Zealand apples to be wholly superior in CO_2-reduction terms than British apples. Its conclusions hinge on the fact that our poorer climate gives lower yields and our more chemical- and fuel-intensive growing techniques need more power: both of these conspire to make a British apple's environmental footprint exceed its Kiwi counterpart by a factor of two, even taking into account the latter's long journey. It is true that shipping, per 'tonne/kilometre', is vastly more efficient than air freight and even a great deal more efficient than road freight, which is why there is little difference in the food-miles impact between an apple from Auckland or Andalucia. However, the NZ report uses a yield figure for British apples that is half what DEFRA (Department for Environment, Food and Rural Affairs) statistics show we are currently achieving, so perhaps it should be taken with a pinch of (organic) salt. Still, the report – and others on similar subjects – illustrates that the food-miles issue is much more complex than often characterized. There is not always a direct relation between distance and eco-devastation. So the concerned apple shopper should not feel too bad about biting into a Braeburn in the April–July period when new-season antipodean imports plug the gap in our own season.

Not even a little bit green:

European imports during the British apple season

Golden Delicious? Never was an apple variety so inappropriately named. Intensity of flavour is often linked to nutritional value: a tasty new-season Discovery has four times the vitamin C of a bland Golden Delicious. It makes neither gastronomic nor ecological sense to eat European imports during our own apple season: British apples offer better variety, better flavour and few food miles.

MORE INFORMATION
Apple day: via www.commonground.org.uk

Apple season

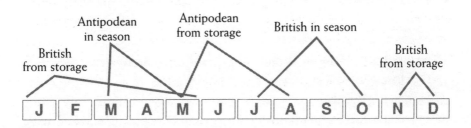

Babies

Any discussion of the greenness of babies should naturally be prefaced with a population-related caveat. If you take the view of some green thinkers that humans are, as far as the Earth is concerned, a pathogenic organism that needs to be controlled, then having any children at all is a pretty un-green thing to do. Population issues apart, having children has a potentially enormous environmental impact. Just the disposable nappies used by a Western infant will create a carbon footprint bigger than that created by all the activities of a developing-world baby. In wealthy countries such as Britain, having babies is the spur for an orgy of consumption that leaves a mighty bootee-print on the planet.

Deep green:
No babies

Ultra-hardcore deep greenies put the Earth first, citing scientist James Lovelock's view that Gaia is suffering from 'disseminated primatemaia' – a plague of people that the planet will eventually shrug off, probably with climate change. To such extremists, adding to, or even maintaining, the planet's human burden is a bad idea. Such self-sacrifice for the greater ecological good may be laudable but unfortunately runs counter to most people's most powerful biological instincts.

Dark green:
The low-impact baby

Food, energy use and travel account for most of a baby's environmental impact. Food is easy to deal with: breastfeeding radically reduces the resource and energy cost of feeding a new baby (see p. 17 for detailed statistics); thereafter, a low-meat diet that avoids processed and packaged foods will keep the food 'footprint' as small as possible. Nappies are major users of resources and energy. A debate rages between environmental campaigners and multinationals about whether disposable or washable is best. The 3 billion disposable nappies chucked away each year are the biggest domestic item in British landfill sites and most take ages to biodegrade. But washable nappies have an environmental cost too, in terms of electricity and water use. Use the greenest modern washing machines (see p. 267 for details), though, and the 'footprint' of washables will be half that of disposables; use a laundry service and it will be lighter still. As for transport, dark green babies will not do a great deal of driving, or if they do it will be in the greenest possible vehicle (see p. 54) or, preferably, on a bicycle or in a hand-me-down pram. And it goes without saying that low-impact babies will have clothes and toys that are either second-hand or made out of renewable and biodegradable materials. However, as any parent knows, even the greenest babies will soon grow up to desire the most lurid and synthetic things in the shop. Children are not natural environmentalists.

Not even a little bit green:
The baby who has everything

There is an almost infinite menu of ways to give your baby a carbon footprint bigger than that of a developing-world village. Bottle-feeding, with all the food production, packaging and transport, then heating and sterilizing it entails, uses vast amounts of energy and resources (see p. 18). Buying highly packaged and processed baby foods is also energy-intensive and creates maximum waste. Why mash a banana when you could buy a ludicrously expensive small jar of indeterminate baby mush? Encouraging baby to have a highly carnivorous diet expands its cute little footprint ever further (see also meat, p. 163). Disposable nappies may consume no water or energy 'in use', but their manufacture is highly resource-intensive and involves unpleasant chemicals. Naturally, the baby who has everything must be protected from the rigours of the outside world, so its parents will crank up the household thermostat and ensure that most of its travels are in the safe cocoon of a large car or, for the very shortest journeys, in the beefiest baby buggy available. And of course baby's arrival will stimulate the purchase of a huge range of absolutely essential gadgets and gizmos, from battery-powered rocking chairs to sophisticated baby alarms.

MORE INFORMATION
Real nappy campaign: www.realnappycampaign.com

Baby milk

You could argue that there are multiple shades of green in the world of baby milk. Organic infant formula, for example, may have a marginally lighter ecological footprint than stuff derived from conventionally grown ingredients. There may be differences of environmental impact between packaging, production or the provenance of the fifty or so ingredients in the many competing formula brands. But whilst this book may be predicated on the notion that 'being green is never black and white', baby milk is one area of modern life where there are no environmental nuances.

Deep green:
Breastmilk

'If a multinational company developed a product that was a nutritionally balanced and delicious food, a wonder drug that both prevented and treated disease, cost almost nothing to produce and could be delivered in quantities controlled by the consumers' needs, the very announcement of their find would send their shares rocketing to the very top of the stock market.' This introduction to breastmilk in Gabrielle Palmer's *The Politics of Breastfeeding* neatly captures the nutritional, economic and therefore ecological issues surrounding it. Look very hard for any environmental impacts of breastmilk and you could contend that the presence of certain persistent environmental pollutants in human breastmilk might be cause for concern; or maybe that the increased calorific requirements (and thirst) of breastfeeding mothers increases the overall human demand for food and water. But these issues are more than cancelled out by the myriad well-documented health benefits of breastmilk and the fact that it requires no energy-intensive manufacturing, packaging or transporting.

Not even a little bit green:
Formula milk

At birth, 69 per cent of babies in the UK are breastfed, but by six months – the age up to which the World Health Organization recommends babies should be fed nothing but breastmilk – this has fallen to just 21 per cent. As a result, the babies born in our country each year get through 12.75 million kilos of infant formula in their first six months, at a total cost to their parents of at least £90 million. This is big business, the environmental 'externalities' of which include 14 million or so items of metal or plastic packaging to be recycled, landfilled or burned; the fuel costs of transporting thousands of tonnes of product; and the boiling and use of 75 million litres of drinking water. Most significant of all are the impacts of the agriculture needed to create the dairy and plant-oil products that are the principal ingredients of infant formula. But the main reason formula is consigned to this category is that nearly all of these impacts are unnecessary. We largely do not need the ecological disaster that is infant formula milk because there is an infinitely superior and environmentally benign substitute. Fewer than 3 per cent of women are physiologically incapable of breastfeeding: the factors that dissuade many others from doing so today are a complex, potent mix of the cultural and economic. For example, for every £20 spent per baby by food companies marketing infant formula milks, only 14 pence is spent promoting breastfeeding. A return to widespread breast-feeding would be good news for the planet as well as its infant human inhabitants.

MORE INFORMATION
The National Childbirth Trust: www.nct.org.uk
Baby Milk Action: www.babymilkaction.org

Bananas

Bananas are huge. The most popular fruit in Britain, their sales are worth three-quarters of a billion pounds a year in this country alone. For supermarkets, they are the most valuable food item, exceeded in money-making power only by lottery tickets and fuel. Globally, they are the fourth most important staple crop and a crucial source of export income for at least fifteen Latin American and Caribbean countries: the Windward Islands, for example, are highly dependent on banana exports to Britain. With this much money at stake, there's bound to be an environmental downside. It's not all in the transport: bananas rack up plenty of food miles but at least they are delivered by sea, where pollution per tonne/kilometre is a hundred times less severe than air-freighting. With bananas, it's the cultivation that's the problem. Grow them on a large, monocultural scale, which is the tempting thing to do if you are a big company looking to maximize profits, and finicky, disease-prone banana plants need major doses of agrochemicals.

Deep green:
Fairtrade organic bananas

If the definition of 'green' in this book is all about environmental impact (see introduction, p. 1), then banana denial should be the greenest choice on account of all the food miles, refrigeration, artificial ethylene ripening and so on. Or should it? Thanks to various unsavoury twists and turns of colonial history, several national economies are now utterly dependent on the banana trade. If we stopped buying, what would they do? Start growing coca (see p. 102)? Start wars? Whatever might happen, there's a strong chance it could be less green than growing bananas. It's not exactly scientific to speculate in this way, but the banana trade is an illustration of how greenness is often more complex than just looking at measurable environmental impacts. It may well be that supporting 'best-practice' banana-growing is a sound ecological investment. As with other developing-country commodities, Fairtrade guarantees a decent price for producers. And organic production, though tricky with bananas, eliminates the heavy agrochemical use and is better for biodiversity and the environment of the banana-growing regions.

Dark green:
Fairtrade or organic bananas

No need for hand-wringing at the shelves if you can't find bananas that are both Fairtrade and organic: either option is good. Fairtrade bananas are very unlikely to have been produced on a large and destructive scale. So whilst they are produced with some energy-intensive and polluting agrochemicals, it will be at a level that is likely to be much lower than for 'standard' bananas. Organic bananas may not have been fairly traded, but their production will be on a scale that is more likely to be benefiting small producers directly. Soil fertility comes from natural fertilizers, weeds are controlled manually and pests controlled with a range of non-chemical strategies. There is, however, a banana disease (Black Sigatoka) that can only be treated with increasingly heavy doses of fungicide: where this disease is present, organic banana production is impossible.

 Bananas

Not even a little bit green:
Any old banana

After cotton (see p. 70) bananas are the second most sprayed crop in the world. When cultivated on large-scale plantations, they get regular doses (delivered by aeroplane or by hand) of herbicides, fungicides and insecticides to keep at bay the various maladies that can afflict the banana plant. The banana bunches themselves are often wrapped on the tree with pesticide-coated plastic bags for protection. Five of the chemicals used on bananas are classified as 'extremely hazardous' by the World Health Organization; and three organophosphate pesticides are applied that are not approved for use in the UK. On large plantations, which are mostly run by the four corporations that manage 80 per cent of world banana trade, more money is spend on agrochemicals than on workers' wages. All of this puts stresses on watercourses and on human health; and there are numerous lawsuits outstanding in relation to workers having been affected by the agrochemicals used in banana cultivation. Of samples of bananas delivered to UK schools in 2005, all contained pesticide residues at or below the maximum allowable level and two-thirds had residues of multiple agrochemicals, a threefold increase on samples tested in 2004. Any old banana is likely to have been produced by one of the large US corporations that have lobbied for a global free market in bananas: this will tip the balance in favour of the big guys and threatens small producers in fragile, banana-dependent economies such as the Windward Islands. Careless banana-purchasing could, ultimately, cost lives.

MORE INFORMATION
Campaign for a sustainable banana: www.bananalink.org.uk

Barbecues

As our climate warms, so the primal practice of outdoor cooking becomes more and more popular in a country whose summers seemed once too dismal. As pungent smoke engulfs your washing line on sunny weekends, it's difficult to think environmentally positive thoughts about barbecues. But it is perfectly possible to have a sustainable, carbon-neutral barbecue, although what you slap on it (see in particular meat, p. 163, and fish, p. 114) will have as important an impact as the fuel you use.

Deep green:
Solar stove

Without fire or smoky flavours, this is the 'no fun' outdoor cooking option. Solar stoves mainly work by using reflectors to direct the sun's heat at a dark pot, creating the perfect conditions for slow cooking. It's hard to imagine much jolly conviviality being created around a static, weird-looking contraption that needs none of the fire-management skills that so engage men in the barbecue process. On the upside, though, short of having access to your own geothermal vent, this is the most environmentally benign way of cooking bar none.

Dark green:
Using well-dried waste wood or local coppiced wood

Charcoal (see below) can be a low-impact fuel source but wood is even greener. It needs no processing, although lengthy drying (a year or more) will make for a much more efficient burn. Unlike fossil fuels, burning wood does not add to the net stock of CO_2 in the atmosphere; however it does release particulates and volatile organic compounds (VOCs), atmospheric pollutants that are good neither for health nor the neighbour's washing. Using waste wood from near to where you live minimizes the transport costs of what is, after all, a heavy fuel. However, for cooking purposes, choosing natural waste wood rather than old planks that may have been treated with preservatives is the healthiest option. If there is a sustainable source of coppiced wood nearby (maybe from your own small patch of trees) then that too will keep the barbie's footprint to a minimum.

Quite green:
Locally sourced charcoal

Charcoal has around twice the 'energy density' of wood, so provides a much more efficient heat source and burns more cleanly. However, its production, in which wood is heated in the absence of air to drive out the moisture and other volatile substances, does itself use energy. But given that 90 per cent of barbecue charcoal sold in the UK comes from overseas, often from tropical forests, much of charcoal's environmental impact comes from transportation. Buying locally is a good way to reduce your barbie's impact. Much local charcoal comes from wood that has been coppiced, a very sustainable practice that produces attractive and biodiverse woodland, and encourages local 'craft' businesses: both coppicing and charcoal-burning are highly skilled activities that can bring employment to rural areas.

Light green:
FSC-certified charcoal

It has the fuel miles but not the sustainability issues. Charcoal that carries the Forest Stewardship Council logo will at least have come from forests that are sustainably managed rather than simply clear-cut to provide the fuel for your sausages. FSC-certified charcoal is now widely available; however, beware FSC briquettes (see below for more on briquettes): they may derive from sustainable wood but may also contain some environmental nasties.

Pale green:
Propane

Gas barbecues are not really green at all. They are burning a fossil fuel, so contributing net CO_2 to the atmosphere; and the cylinders they use have to be manufactured and trucked around, making them much less efficient than cooking on mains gas. And the swankiest models can use as much energy as an industrial space heater. The one advantage gas barbies do have is that they burn more cleanly, kicking out a hundred times less carbon monoxide than briquettes and creating much less of the particulate and VOC pollution that wood- or charcoal-burning creates.

Not particularly green:
Briquettes

At least one half of the population enjoys the fire-lighting rituals around barbecuing; but many men like to eliminate any risk that their pyrotechnic prowess might be called into question. Barbecue briquettes are the answer. Often impregnated with lighter fuel and made of a mix of charcoal and coal dust, they light easily and burn hotter and for longer. This convenience comes at an environmental cost: briquette emissions are nastier (and their fuel content won't help the taste or healthiness of your food, either) and they lose green points for containing fossil fuels too.

Not even a little bit green:
Disposable barbecue with briquettes

Cheap, quick and easy – but a bit of a nightmare from a strictly environmental perspective. Disposable barbecues have all the disadvantages of briquettes plus all the downsides of unnecessary waste. They could, in theory, be recycled – but their name doesn't exactly encourage users to do this.

MORE INFORMATION
Sustainable charcoal: via www.bioregional.com

Baths

Taking a bath has had a bad ecological press for a while now, on account of the fact that the average bath uses 80 litres of water, which takes about 3.4kWh of energy to heat. So that's over half the average daily British water use (see also water, p. 276) and, if your water is heated by gas (electricity is more than twice as bad), 650 grams of CO_2 emitted, just for a nice soak. However, thanks to lovely luxury technology that makes them consume more and more water, showers (see p. 226) are catching up with baths and threatening to usurp their position as the second biggest household water guzzlers after the dreaded toilet (see p. 251). And some of the green options for taking a bath are decidedly more convivial than those for showering, because a shower's comfort is almost always in direct performance to its water and energy use.

Deep green:
Go jump in a river

What are you, some kind of softie? For the hardest of the hardcore, bathing is a non-essential use of a precious resource. And imagine carrying 80 litres of water from the stream to the tipi: it's just a waste of energy that could otherwise be used to chop down trees or hunt things. Then there's the kilo or so of dry wood that will be needed to heat the water up. We managed without daily baths for millennia; and millions still do, so why bother? Far easier just to take the plunge from time to time.

Dark green:
Bathing in solar-/biofuel-heated rainwater

If you must have a bath, then heating it with renewable energy and using harvested rainwater at least makes the process 'resource-neutral'. There are plenty of solar hot-water, wood-burning and rain-harvesting technologies (see pp. 137, 139 and 277) around to make this possible and it would of course make sense for your bathing to be part of a 'whole house' solar/biofuel/rain-harvesting strategy. Unless you are already set up for solar hot water, wood-burning and rain harvesting, the carbon-neutral bath does come at a cost: and a family of four will need maybe a quarter of a tonne of wood a year just to heat the bathwater when the sun doesn't shine. Still, what could be cosier than sun-kissed or wood-fired rainwater?

Quite green:
Sharing

Two average showers will use as much water and, if they are electrically heated, result in more CO_2 emissions than an average bath. If they are power showers, they will use a great deal more water. So climbing into the bath together, or in sequence, depending on the occasion, is a great wheeze for saving both water and energy. And if the water is still warm when you're done, leaving it in till it's cold means it will carry on radiating heat: depending on the layout of your house, this could make a useful contribution on a cold evening.

Light green:
Funny shapes

Peanut-shaped or tapered baths will provide a similar bathing space for less water. So if you're considering a new 'green' bathroom, weird-shaped baths are worth a look, as long as they are not too big.

Not even a little bit green:
Monster whirlpool bath

At the top end of the market, there really is no limit to how your bath can trash the planet. There's the option of energy-intensive metals or rare hardwoods, for example; but for real eco-hooliganism it has to be the monster whirlpool bath with massage jets, warm air jets, lighting, even an integrated TV and FM radio. With 400+ litres capacity you will at least be able to share with room to spare, but any meagre brownie points earned by doing that will be well and truly obliterated by the behemoth's vast water and energy use.

Beans

Deducing the relative greenness of beans is a tricky business, on account of how diverse a foodstuff they are. The many different species of edible bean can arrive in our kitchens fresh, dried, tinned, frozen or hidden away in the depths of processed foods. How they arrive in our kitchen has a major bearing on whether or not they clobber the planet, for example whether it's by sea, air or a short walk from the garden. And whilst we might castigate that iconic eco-nasty, the air-freighted fresh green haricot bean, for its mighty output of CO_2 per gram, is the dried bean that undergoes ages of soaking and slow cooking before it can be deemed edible any better? The key issue with beans is seasonality. The natural, outdoor season for fresh beans in Britain runs from around May to September, kicking off with broad beans and ending with runners. This means we have to do without outdoor-grown fresh beans for more than half the year, so indoor growing and air-freighting now fill the seasonal gap.

Deep green:
Your own beans

Beans are one of the easiest backyard crops to grow and they have the additional benefit of fixing nitrogen at their roots, thus adding fertility to your soil. Grow a mix, say, of broad, French and runner varieties and you can have fresh beans in the garden for the whole growing season. Hardcore self-sufficiency types might want to dry or freeze late-season beans to add to hearty winter dishes, because they certainly won't be cheating the seasons with imports.

Dark green:
Seasonal, local, and organic if you can get it

From June to September it should be possible to find British beans, although farmers' markets and local greengrocers may be a better bet than supermarkets. Beans from not much further afield in Europe are also available until October. Minimizing food miles for beans is about eating quality as much as the environment: beans of all kinds degrade quickly after picking, so the shortest plot-to-plate distance is the best. Non-organic beans are less pesticide-intensive than other crops and this is reflected in residues, which recent surveys found in only 15–30 per cent of samples.

Quite green:
Dried beans

This is the old-fashioned way of ensuring that the high-protein nutrition a bean provides is available throughout the year. Just how eco-friendly dried beans are is slightly moot, in that they need a great deal of water and energy-intensive cooking in order to become edible. As yet there exists no 'life cycle analysis' pitting the dried bean's eco-credentials against those of, say, the air-freighted out-of-season bean. So this is by necessity a subjective placing, based on all the other impacts and consequences of the air-freighted variety (see p. 32).

Pale green:
Baked beans

Interesting baked-bean facts: they are 'Navy' beans, a variety that doesn't grow well in the UK and is therefore shipped over here from its main growing region in Michigan and neighbouring areas around the Great Lakes. The Heinz factory in Wigan alone cans 1,000 tonnes of such beans a week to meet our demands, which is almost the same as Britons' total consumption of fresh beans. Baked beans get a relatively low ranking because they are a processed food, containing other ingredients that needed resource-intensive growing and processing: for example tomatoes, sugar and syrups and cornflour. And then there are the tins themselves, which, although recyclable, add weight and 'embodied energy' to the humble baked bean.

Not even a little bit green:
Air-freighted fresh beans

Here is where one of the most vexed debates about food and the environment rages. On the one hand, there is no denying the relatively small contribution of air-freighted food to our total greenhouse gas emissions; nor the fact that such trade brings valuable export income to developing countries. On the other hand, emissions from the airborne food trade are growing rapidly. We now import almost as many beans by air from Kenya alone as we produce locally: our imports of green beans have grown fourfold since 1990 whilst UK production has dropped sharply. The 'radiative forcing' effect of air-transport emissions is said to multiply them threefold. And then there's the concept of 'virtual water': because of the water needed to grow crops such as beans, we are, in effect, importing large volumes of water from a region that is water-stressed and likely to become more so as global warming progresses. Overall, the energy demand of an African bean is at least twelve times its seasonal, local counterpart. The casting vote must, however, go to necessity. If we accept that energy use and emissions in relation to food production are an issue, then surely such 'unnecessary' food trade should be considered the least green. It's not as if we can't eat an interesting and varied diet in the UK winter without air-freighted fresh produce. Perhaps we should focus on helping such developing countries to grow export crops that have smaller carbon footprints, rather than insisting on summer produce in the depths of winter.

Not even a little bit green either:
Northern European hothouse beans

If you come across these in the winter, they will not have made a long air journey, nor removed water from a water-stressed region. But they will have been grown with artificial heat, which puts them on a par in energy terms with the air-freighted variety.

Bean season

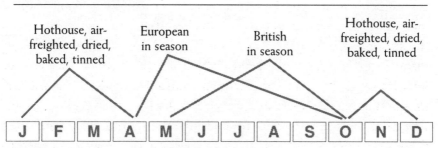

Hothouse, air-freighted, dried, baked, tinned

European in season

British in season

Hothouse, air-freighted, dried, baked, tinned

J F M A M J J A S O N D

Beef

Here's a topic to test those of us whose concern for the environment is matched by our love of a fine steak. Meat in general (see p. 163 and other meat entries) is a very inefficient, resource-intensive way of producing food for people. Beef is the biggest resource-guzzler of the lot, needing the most land and water of all livestock to produce and – on account of vast amounts of methane emitted – making the biggest contribution to global warming. Yes, bovine flatus is helping to change the climate. Huge areas of land are needed just to grow food for cattle, never mind rear them. For example, in the United States it has been estimated that a shift away from grain-fed beef to vegetarianism would mean that crops in the vast Mississippi Basin would need 50 per cent less land and fertilizer. There would be no change to the amount of protein in the human food chain and the worrying hypoxic 'dead zone' in the waters of the Gulf of Mexico, caused by agricultural runoff, would cease to exist. It's hard to make an environmental case for meat-eating at the best of times; doing so for beef is hardest of all. But there is a useful tie-in with health, ethics and economics. Eating too much beef or cheap beef is bad for your health as well as the planet's. The very best beef is packed with nutrients, and reared largely outdoors in a way that maximizes animal welfare whilst reducing its environmental impact as far as possible. It is also very expensive, so for most eco-carnivores it will only ever be an occasional treat.

Deep green:
Very occasional beef, sourced with obsessive care

Extremely careful beef-sourcing is key to both environmental and gastronomic satisfaction. First of all, make sure it's British: our production standards are largely higher than elsewhere in the world and there will be many fewer food miles. Then make sure it is from a suckler herd, which consists of slow-growing beef breeds whose calves start on their mothers' milk then after weaning get the most natural diet. Breeds to look out for include Aberdeen Angus, Hereford, Highland, Sussex, Welsh Black or other rare breeds. Next, find out whether or not it has been fed largely on grass and natural forage. This makes a huge difference to the eating and nutritional quality as well as to the cattle's carbon hoofprint. Finally, if it's organic, then it will have grazed on natural pastures whose grasses have not been grown with energy-intensive artificial fertilizers, potentially adding further to the eating and nutritional quality of the meat. As a bonus, such cattle may also have contributed to maintaining habitats for certain bird species. Phew. Such beef – available at some farmers' markets, direct from producers and at the best butchers – will cost an arm and a leg and thus instantly turn you into a 'beef reducer', which is best from both a health and an ecological point of view.

Quite green:
Occasional supermarket organics

Whilst the outlets listed above will give you the all-important opportunity to interrogate suppliers about the cattle's lifestyle, supermarkets do stock varying degrees of good British beef, although labels need careful scrutiny to make sure that it's not, say, a British breed that has just breezed in from Brazil. In the context of organics it is worth pointing out that, via their manure, cattle are the major alternative source of nitrogen fertilizer after the artificial stuff, which organic systems largely forbid. So without beef, organic agriculture would be difficult. As an illustration, a small-scale commercial organic vegetable operation needs the manure of around eighty cattle to keep its hungry plants happy.

Pale green:
No beef

Although not without their own issues (see pp. 60, 204), chickens and pigs are more efficient converters of food to flesh and are certainly much easier to fit into your back yard if you're interested in DIY options. Now it can of course always be argued that vegetarianism is the truly eco-friendliest option – eating meat has been estimated to account for over 10 per cent of the average personal carbon footprint in the UK – but if you want to remain carnivorous yet green, beef is probably the meat you should cut first for the reasons mentioned above. It can take 100,000 litres of water to produce a kilo of beef, which will itself result in the release of up to 32kg of CO_2-equivalent greenhouse gas into the atmosphere. However, as long as there are dairy cattle there will always be unwanted male calves; and if you are a lacto-vegetarian who would rather these were not shot at birth or exported live for the veal trade, then it's best if someone eats beef.

Not even a little bit green:
Cheap beef

The real problems with beef relate to diet and upbringing. Intensively reared beef is fed largely on concentrated, grain-based feeds with components such as wheat, maize and soya. It is these feeds that take up much of the world's vast acreage of arable crops, often in environmentally sensitive areas, and they are responsible for huge loads of fertilizers and agricultural chemicals. Cows didn't evolve to eat grain, though, and the resulting meat is deficient in omega-3 fatty acids. Cheaper beef is also often a by-product of dairy production: cows need to calve to keep producing milk and are often mated with a beef-producing breed so that the calf can be used productively, even if male. Such dairy-cross calves are removed from their mothers and raised more intensively, often indoors, slaughtered earlier (at 12–18 months rather than 2–4 years for sucklers) and are more likely to be fed compound feeds. It has, however, been estimated that a move away from dairy-related production to 100 per cent suckler-herd beef would in fact double the environmental impact of the meat, because of the economies of scale in the dairy/meat combination. So this puts the omnivorous environmentalist on the horns of a dilemma: more intensification of farming, or less meat and dairy consumption overall?

Beer and lager

*I*n *purely environmental terms, beer is madness. The area of land given over to barley for brewing adds up to hundreds of thousands of hectares which could otherwise be used to grow food crops, create beautiful wildlife reserves, forests, etc. It takes 6 pints of water to brew a pint of beer, in a process that also uses significant amounts of energy and produces effluents as well as 850 kilotonnes of CO_2 per year in the UK. If we all just took the pledge and drank nothing but tap water (see p. 276), the world would be a better place. Or would it? Beer-fuelled humanity has its issues, for sure; but beer-deprived humanity could be bad for the planet as well as bad-tempered. Packaging accounts for one third of beer's environmental impact, with non-returnable glass bottles and cans causing the biggest problems because of the energy needed to make, transport and recycle them. If people are going to drink (which they are, because prohibition on ecological grounds would be the shortest political suicide note in history), then draught beer from big, re-usable barrels, served in re-usable glasses in the convivial, communal surroundings of the pub, is one of the greenest booze choices.*

Deep green:
Go to the pub, drink hand-pulled real ale, preferably organic

Whilst eco-purists may harrumph that the only green booze is no booze, beer purists fond of a good old-fashioned, hand-pulled pint can rejoice in the fact that theirs is the greenest choice. For the reasons mentioned above, draught beer is better because its packaging, distribution and transport costs are lower. 'Real' or cask-conditioned ale gets additional eco-points because its production process does not need the extra chilling and pasteurizing that keg beers require. Nor does it need to be refrigerated in the pub, because it is typically served at cellar temperature. Drinking organic beer means that the barley and hops were grown without energy-intensive agrochemicals, although with only one hectare of organic hops in Britain and a few thousand of organic barley, it is hard to come by and the ingredients may well have racked up a few beer miles.

Dark green:
Homebrew

There are many levels of home brewing, from using simple brewing kits with ready-made malt extract through to replicating the 'real' brewing process that starts with finding and mashing your own barley. The latter, whilst the most natural, uses much more energy but produces a far better product; homebrew from the simplest kits will not need boiling (which is what uses much of the energy in the brewing process) but the end result won't be so close to what you could find in the pub. Despite the energy, water and transportation involved in the beer industry, there are also economies of scale. No one has been nerdy enough to do a 'life cycle analysis' of the energy used in home brewing versus, say, the production of real ale in a traditional brewery. However, it's a fair guess that if we all started trying to replicate pub-quality beer at home, the overall environmental impact would be higher. Our neighbourhoods might smell good, though . . .

Quite green:
Go to the pub and drink any old keg beer

On the face of it, keg beer, the bête noire of the Campaign for Real Ale, is not particularly green. Unlike real ale it is conditioned in the brewery (rather than in the cask) in a process that involves chilling and filtering to remove the yeast, then heating to pasteurize the product. It is then kept in pressurized casks, with bottled nitrogen and CO_2 putting back the fizz that the production process took out. To add insult to ecological injury, the beer then needs additional refrigeration to get it down to a typical serving temperature of 5°C. Lager gets an even poorer green rating because it is fermented at lower temperatures and thus needs even more refrigeration. However, the materials and machinery for canning and bottling (and transporting, recycling or disposing of the bottles and cans) add significantly to the 'embodied energy' of beer. So even if it is the Watney's Red Barrel of the real-ale enthusiast's worst nightmares, because it's still in big, re-usable barrels and served in re-usable glasses, keg beer is not yet at the bottom of the green scale.

Pale green:
Local beer in cans or bottles

Two studies of beer's environmental impact have concluded that because of the energy needed to make them, glass bottles are the worst form of packaging, beating even aluminium cans. However, drink beer from as nearby as possible and at least the beer miles will be reduced; drink organic beer, which is more readily available in bottles than on draught, and the effect of the bottle's contents on the environment is reduced yet further. Returnable bottle and can schemes make the whole 'staying away from the pub' thing a more eco-friendly proposition: these have yet to catch on in the UK but are common in some European countries, especially Denmark and Finland.

Not even a little bit green:
Exotic, imported bottled lager from far away

The least green beers are the ones that have racked up the most beer miles, on top of being in eco-unfriendly bottles and having been produced in the most energy-inefficient way. We're making good headway on this in Britain: lager, with its extra need for refrigeration in both brewery and pub, is forecast to account for 80 per cent of all beer volume by 2010; and we are already net importers of beer, despite being extremely good at making it. Read the label carefully if you want to check your beer is doing the maximum damage: many foreign-labelled beers are brewed under licence in the UK, which drastically reduces the beer miles.

More Information
The Campaign for Real Ale: www.camra.org.uk

Bicycles

Aren't all bicycles green? Pretty much. Cycling is the most energy-efficient form of transport available: you go up to five times faster for the same effort as walking. Despite this ultra-greenness, a pro-car commentator has tried to show that because of the CO_2 emitted by people exercising, a car full of sedentary passengers would in fact be more environmentally friendly than walkers (and by extension cyclists) over a given distance. What the writer failed to point out was that the car uses a fossil fuel, releasing ancient, stored carbon and therefore adding net CO_2 to the atmosphere. The person, on the other hand, is carbon-neutral, fuelled by food that has already absorbed carbon whilst growing. So don't worry about adding to the greenhouse effect as you pant your way to work. And unlike the car, the bicycle emits minimal other pollutants, makes hardly any noise and takes much less energy to build.

Still, no matter how green and groovy bikes are, there's no escaping the fact that all sorts of energy-intensive processes are needed to get them into the shop window. From aluminium production to shipping, bikes have an environmental impact. Sure, it's minimal compared to a car, but we're being picky here.

Deep green:
Second-hand bike

Buy a second-hand bike and you prolong its life, save it from landfill and don't use any new natural resources. Second-hand bikes can cost next to nothing and are often a better buy than the cheapest brand-new bikes, which have shoddy, short-lived components. However, second-hand machines can also be nicked, and a bit knackered. So it's best to try before you buy, looking for the biggest problems which, in order of magnitude and financial pain are: a wrong-sized, bent, dented or cracked frame; worn or damaged gears, cogs or brakes; damaged wheels; and loose handlebars or stem.

Dark green:
Wooden bike

If you happen to be in, say, Congo or Uganda, around $30 buys you a *chokoudou*, made from local wood and with recycled rubber tyres. As it's a scooter rather than a bicycle, riding it back home will be a challenge. But few will be able to match you for individuality and eco-friendliness on the morning commute. If you have a small child, the wooden 'Like-a-Bike' and its imitators (also without pedals) are the perfect way for infants to get around whilst learning the hardest bit of cycling, balance. At the high-tech end of the renewable materials scale, there are niche producers making bikes out of bamboo. This ultra-strong, natural, shock-absorbing material is used with stuff like carbon fibre to produce bikes that are both beautiful and (relatively) sustainable. And riding a bike which is, in essence, made of grass has just got to be green.

Quite green:
Steel bike

Once, most bike frames were made of steel. Today, the majority of new bikes in our shops are made of aluminium alloy (see below for the reason). Steel beats aluminium for eco-friendliness on several grounds. Whilst – as a visit to somewhere like Port Talbot will confirm – steel production may not exactly be all flowers and fluffiness, it uses a third of the energy of aluminium production, so a steel bike has less 'embodied energy'. Steel frames have a longer lifespan because they don't fatigue over time like aluminium; they are less likely to break and more likely to be repairable if they do. So your steel bike should last a lifetime: and the extra weight in a steel frame becomes a problem only if you are starting to get competitive with your cycling.

Light green:
Aluminium bikes

If it's got big fat frame tubes, then it's probably made of aluminium. Aluminium is softer than steel, but much lighter, so the bigger tubes provide strength but don't make the bike heavy. The reason that most bikes today are aluminium is all to do with robots. Thicker tubes are easy for these tireless chaps to weld, making mass production much cheaper. As a material, aluminium loses to steel on the green front because it takes much more energy to produce. (At the time of writing, a large area of Iceland is about to be flooded to create the hydropower needed to run an aluminium smelter.) And although much aluminium is recycled, only 'virgin' metal can be used in bike frames. Also, because most mass production of frames happens in the Far East, aluminium bikes are most likely to have made a long journey to the shop. The frames have a finite lifespan because they fatigue over time; and if broken, they're almost impossible to fix.

Light green 2:
Carbon-fibre or titanium bikes

These splendid high-tech materials make for ultra-light and comfortable, if expensive, bicycles. The difficulty of titanium welding means there is a lot of wastage in the process; and whilst carbon-fibre bikes are at least made out of the substance that so troubles the world at the moment, their construction does involve noxious resins and adhesives.

Pale green:
Electric bikes

Whilst they may manage the equivalent of 800–2,000 m.p.g., electric bikes are near the bottom end of the bicycle green scale. They have eco-unfriendly batteries, need power and are bigger and heavier than normal bikes. Yet however much hardcore cyclists like the author might sneer at them on these grounds – and at the fact that they seem destined never to be even remotely cool – if electric bikes tempt some people out of cars, they can't be all bad.

Not even a little bit green:
Nothing

No bicycles fall into this category, because however they are made, bikes are still the most energy-efficient, lowest-impact form of land transport, with a list of environmental, social and personal benefits as long as the Tour de France. So unless your bike is made of plutonium, there's really not much you can do to kill the planet with it.

MORE INFORMATION
Second-hand bike buyers' checklist: via www.lcc.org.uk

Boats and ships

The environmental impact of waterborne travel is not exactly top of everyone's list of issues. But with flying (see p. 5) getting so much flak for pumping out disproportionately vast quantities of greenhouse gases per passenger, is it better to take the slow boat? The answer is . . . it depends on the boat and what it's carrying. For some applications, shipping is far more eco-friendly than the alternatives. Per tonne-kilometre, sea freight can kick out a third of the CO_2 of road freight and a mere one per cent of the emissions that air freight produces. But when it comes to shipping people, the equations change. Fast boats, with relatively few passengers, travelling over long distances make even airliners look frugal by comparison.

Deep green:
Sailing

At last, a deep green pursuit that doesn't involve too much self-denial. Now clearly there are shades of sailing greenness, mostly in direct proportion to expenditure. At the top end of the market, exotic hardwoods, all manner of high-tech materials and powerful auxiliary engines will knock the green spots off your sailing boat; and anyway, if you can afford such a thing, environmental considerations may not be uppermost in your mind. But something relatively simple (even something home-made, if you're really brave) will cover long distances with minimal use of fuel. Wind and solar will keep the batteries charged, assuming you're not too green to eschew electronic gadgets like GPS receivers. Provided you reach your destination – sailing on the open ocean is not without risks – you will be arriving with a clear eco-conscience.

Dark green:
Alternative-fuel boats

As yet, these are in their infancy and mostly suitable for very specific (and short) journeys. Solar/electric launches ply Lake Coniston in the Lake District; a plug-in 'eco-catamaran' potters around coastal Cornwall; and a small solar ferry travels, very slowly, around the Serpentine in London. A shipping company is developing a zero-emission vessel concept powered by wind, solar and wave power (although ironically it is designed to carry 10,000 cars: let's hope they're pedal-powered). With realistic non-fossil shipping alternatives still years away, sticking on some tried and tested sails still seems like the best option.

Quite green:
Slow boats, preferably carrying freight

As anyone who has attempted butterfly stroke will know, shifting water is a difficult business. The faster you go, the harder it gets. Conventional passenger boats (which have a maximum speed of 24 knots or less) are never particularly frugal, but they use thirteen times less fuel than a high-speed ferry (30+ knots; see below). So taking the old, slow ferry rather than the fast and racy new one will mean less fuel per passenger. This is an option for long-distance travel too. Several freight lines offer passenger accommodation at reasonable prices: if you don't mind taking fourteen days or so to get to the United States, for example, the prices compare favourably with airfares. Seeing as the freighter will be lugging the containers whether you choose to board or not, your impact on the environment will be negligible. And with ocean-going trade predicted to triple by 2020, there should hopefully be plenty of cabins available.

Not particularly green:
Great big cruise liners

The statistics surrounding modern cruise liners are quite staggering. Plug one into a large town and it would generate all the electricity the place needed. The QE2, which is far from the biggest liner these days, is said to consume around 400 tonnes of heavy fuel oil (HFO) per day. It's worth a mention at this point that HFO, which is a refinery by-product not dissimilar to road tar, is not subject to anything like the pollutant restrictions of road fuels: it is estimated that cargo shipping will account for 75 per cent of all Europe's sulphur dioxide emissions by 2010. Anyway, this gargantuan appetite for fuel translates to around 10 litres per hour for every passenger and means that per-person CO_2 emissions on a transatlantic crossing will exceed those created by flying.

Even less green:
High-speed ferries

Amazingly, thanks to their relatively slow speed and greater passenger capacity, modern cruise liners can offer better overall fuel consumption than high-speed ferries. The sheer effort of propelling a large vessel and its cargo of cars and people at speeds up to and over 40 knots takes astounding amounts of power, which means vast quantities of fuel. The recently withdrawn HSS *Stena Discovery*, which operated from Harwich to Hook of Holland, used as much fuel as all of the line's seven conventional North Sea ships put together.

Not even a little bit green:
Personal motor yacht

The super-rich generally have carbon footprints to match their bank balances. But if you really want to keep up with the environmentally destructive Joneses, you'll need to get a serious motor yacht (as well, of course, as a large private jet, see p. 8). Leaving aside the rare, beautiful and non-renewable natural resources needed to build a decent gin palace, just the fuel it needs will propel you into the carbon-footprint premiership. A four-berth, 60-foot, ultra-luxurious, high-speed yacht with a 2,200-horsepower engine will get through 320 litres of marine diesel per hour, which adds up to a potential 80 litres per hour per passenger, making a luxury liner look like the eco-friendly choice.

MORE INFORMATION
Travel on a cargo ship: www.freightercruises.com

Bread

Sorting out the greenest loaf is a tricky business. Is it the organic one? Maybe: but with Britain growing a mere 15,000 hectares of organic wheat, half of the organic loaves you buy will be made with imported flour, adding food miles. Is it the home-baked one? Possibly: but with an oven guzzling nearly 2kWh of energy just to bake a loaf, bakeries and factories can be more energy-efficient at baking. Whichever it is, bread has a serious impact on the environment, as befits its status as a major food staple. Growing wheat is an energy-intensive business, as is carting around the 2.9 million tonnes of bread we eat each year. So what is the greenest loaf?

Deep green:
Your own bread, baked in a wood oven

Strictly for hardcore smallholders. To grow enough wheat for flour to keep a family in, say, six loaves a week you will need around 500 square metres of land (five times the size of an average garden) and some serious wheat-growing, threshing and milling skills and gear. For the ultimate carbon-neutral, biosphere-friendly loaf, the baking should happen courtesy of biofuels, probably wood (from a sustainable source, of course – maybe your own coppiced woodland, which will take up another hectare or so). You can grow your own yeast, but any sugar and salt will have to be bought in, unless you are also into sugar-beet processing and live by the sea. This thought experiment (which is what it will be for most of us) at least serves to illustrate why it is that an innocent loaf of bread can have such a big eco-footprint.

Dark green:
Organic, home-baked, stoneground, baked in big batches

Sounds pretty groovy, but this option's dark green status is a matter of opinion rather than clear-cut fact. The main debate is around organic flour. Firstly, it may well be imported: although we are 80 per cent self-sufficient in bread wheat, less than one per cent of UK-grown wheat is organic, so half of the organic flour to meet current demand has to come from overseas. Plus there's the inescapable fact that, whilst it takes only two-thirds of the energy to grow (mainly because artificial fertilizers are not used), organic wheat needs two to three times as much land in order to achieve the same yield. But then there are other issues that need to be considered if we're getting deep into the detail, which we are: organic production is better for biodiversity, the decline of which has coincided with the rise of conventional agriculture and its heavy use of herbicides and pesticides. And in the 2005 report of the Pesticides Residue Committee, 90 per cent of samples of 'ordinary' bread contained residues of pesticides: not at levels that are considered harmful, but residues none the less. However, whether organic wheat is, overall, strictly greener at the moment remains difficult to judge and its position here is a subjective one. As for home baking, it can easily beat bakery or industrial bread in energy terms as long as you get the quantity right (see below). Stoneground flour comes from a less industrialized process and results in flour that retains its natural nutrients.

Quite green:

Stoneground organic from the nice local artisan baker down the road

The nice local artisan baker down the road gets knocked into third place by the sheer controllability of home-baked bread. Buy the lovely artisanal stoneground flour from a farmers' market – to which you have cycled, naturally – and the food miles could only be shorter if you grew your own wheat. At around 2kWh per bread-baking session, home baking is bad news if you make one loaf at a time: the bakery can manage on around half a kilowatt hour per loaf. Bung in four or more at a time, though, and you'll beat the baker for energy use but you'll probably be either selling or giving away bread. If you're not into home bread-making, then should you be lucky enough to live near one, the nice, small-scale, local baker is the next best bet.

Light green:

Stoneground conventional bread baked at home or down the road

Even if you can't get hold of right-on speciality flours, home baking still gets green points for energy use because by buying flour and creating bread at home you are cutting down on loaf miles and also potentially saving baking energy. Bread baked in the local bakery is not far behind in green terms because, unlike pre-packaged loaves, its production won't have racked up a high mileage.

Not even a little bit green:
'Sliced and wrapped' industrially produced bread

Much has been written about the nutritional and gastronomic consequences of the Chorleywood Bread Process, by which the majority of British bread is produced. The high-speed milling that precedes this process strips natural nutrients out of the flour which then have to be artificially added back into the bread; then the process itself introduces potentially harmful fats – and other additives – into the bread before finally creating an inferior end product. Environmentally, industrial bread is a bit of a nightmare too. Over 80 per cent of our bread is made in just eleven 'plant bakeries', which burn 5kWh of energy per kilo of bread products. Every day, 7 million loaves leave such vast facilities to be trucked around the country, racking up loaf miles that ultimately contribute to industrial bread's annual tally of 8 tonnes of CO_2 emissions per household. Each week, 50 million polythene wrappers have to be disposed of and because of the difficulty of recycling them, most go to landfill. The bread industry points out that such wrapping is the most efficient choice and is anyway essential to shelf-life and hygiene. Its preferred disposal solution? Pointing out that plastic wrappers have an energy density similar to fuel oil, it suggests incinerating them in an 'energy from waste' plant. As long as all the bread-industry executives advocating this approach are happy to buy up and move into all the property downwind of such a plant, then this sounds like a workable solution. Still not very green, though.

Cars

After water- and space-heating, transport is the next biggest domestic energy user and cars the major contributor to the transport total. With average annual British personal car mileage at 5,545, each of us puts nearly 1.5 tonnes of CO_2 into the air each year from driving alone, which is about 15 per cent of our average carbon footprint and more than half of what some consider our annual carbon allowance should really be. CO_2 aside, the car stands accused of a long list of other eco-crimes, from effects on respiratory health to out-of-control road-building, noise pollution and the rest. So is the sustainable future completely car-free? Or can we have our automotive cake and eat it? Because it should not be forgotten – as it often is by environmentalists – that as well as being apocalyptically destructive, cars can be extremely useful and tremendous fun: and their owners are attached to them with visceral emotion. There are green options: but sadly none of the sort that will excite the visceral emotion brigade. That said, belonging to a car-sharing scheme and doing a few track days in a hired Ferrari will be greener – and probably a great deal less stressful – than being traffic-bound in the latest expensive silver executive chariot.

Deep green:

No car

Whichever way you look at it, this is by far the greenest option. Forgo four wheels and you cease to emit all that pollution, cause no congestion, are no longer responsible for the extraction of all the resources that go into making a car and present no murderous danger to pedestrians and cyclists. You also save a load of money: car owner-ship is estimated to cost between £2,500 and £4,000 per year on average. The problem, of course, is what to do instead. Deep gree-nies who have run for the hills will find the prospect of the 45-mile bicycle round trip to the newsagent taxing, even if the money car-freedom has liberated will buy a serious bike and still leave change for a lightweight trailer to carry the shopping. The fact is that car-free lifestyles work best in cities, where public transport networks are best and everything you need is within easy walking or cycling distance.

Dark green:
Electric with renewable-energy recharging

About 25 per cent of the pollution caused by cars and 20 per cent of the energy expended by them is 'embodied', that is, accounted for by their manufacture. The rest happens during their use. So if you do have a car, making sure that driving it creates minimal environmental impact is the next greenest thing to do. And if greenhouse gases and pollution are the key green issue, then – sorry, petrolheads – electric cars are the next best option. They may not, as some claim, be 'zero-emission': the G-Wiz, for example, emits 66 grams of CO_2 per kilometre, about 40 per cent of the UK average. But if you charge it from your own renewable supply, or that provided by a proper 'green-tariff' operator' (see p. 111), then this (largely) goes away. It's hard to see how current technologies can get closer to carbon-neutral, low-emission motoring than an electric car. However, with a 40 m.p.h. top speed and limited range between charges, the G-Wiz is only really suitable for cities, where cars are least necessary and where it will do little more than create eco-friendly congestion. Bicycles (see p. 42) are cheaper and a lot more fun.

Quite green:
Waste veg-oil power

For about £1,000, most diesels – even high-tech, high-performance ones – can be converted to run on pure vegetable oil. The stuff from the supermarket will work fine, although extra-virgin olive oil is clearly not going to be cost-effective. As pure veg oil is minimally processed and not a fossil fuel, it adds little net CO_2 to the atmosphere. However, the problem with biofuels in general – veg oil, biodiesel, ethanol – is sustainability. Rapeseed oil, the best biofuel bet in a temperate climate, yields around 1,200 litres of oil per hectare. About 30 per cent of the 30 million vehicles on Britain's roads are diesel-powered. If all of these switched to pure veg oil, we would need 12 million hectares of oilseed rape to fuel them, which exceeds Britain's total arable land area by a factor of two. There is therefore a fear that much biodiesel, which is veg oil that has been processed to work in unconverted diesels, will be sourced from higher-yielding tropical crops such as the oil palm, resulting in catastrophic rainforest devastation. And the amount of energy needed to grow and process ethanol (for petrol-engined cars) from maize largely outweighs any CO_2 savings and encourages massive monoculture and GM crop development. So biofuels are very tricky. But waste veg oil from catering businesses might as well be put to good use, and pouring it into a car which would otherwise use a fossil fuel is not a bad idea at all. The legal hurdles involved are tiresome but not insurmountable, and as long as your waste oil is free or cheap, the total cost – including the taxman's share – compares favourably with fossil fuels.

Light green:

Car sharing, low mileage

There's no point shelling out on a fancy hybrid with a view to serious greenness if you're going to be driving everywhere alone and doing serious mileage (see 'Not even a little bit green' below). Sharing instantly reduces the per capita impact of car use and can even be entertaining, although not if fellow occupants fail to share your taste in music, radio stations or conversation. There's a growing spectrum of car-sharing options, from tailoring your car use so it's just for family trips, to informal community car-sharing schemes, online lift-sharing clubs and 'by the hour' car hire.

Pale green:

Low mileage, tiny diesel

Small, modern, diesel-engined cars offer the best CO_2 performance of all the fossil-fuel options and the most frugal have only marginally higher emissions than much-hyped petrol hybrids. Whilst diesels emit lower levels of carbon monoxide and hydrocarbons than petrol engines, they do however kick out more nitrogen oxide and particulates, both of which are harmful to health. Diesels for traffic-bound city driving are therefore not the best choice: but if most of your (limited, of course) miles are on rural roads or motorways, then a small diesel, which – compared to a hybrid – is light, long-lived, reliable and relatively uncomplicated in terms of technology and manufacture, is the 'least worst' option.

Pale green 2:
Low mileage, hybrid

Petrol/electric hybrids offer relatively low CO_2 emissions plus the benefit of low emissions in town, mainly because their engines switch off when stationary. They are technically complex, though; have expensive batteries which will ultimately need replacing; and over long distances don't necessarily perform as well as diesels because the less fuel-efficient petrol engine does most of the work. But hybrids beat diesels for town driving as they will produce fewer toxic emissions when stuck in traffic jams, which, let's face it, is what town driving is all about.

Pale green 3:
Low mileage, LPG

Liquefied petroleum gas offers one big benefit that the first two of our pale green options don't: it's cheap, currently about half the price of petrol or diesel thanks to lower excise duty. LPG conversions cost from £1,600, allow your car to run on petrol or the gas, but put an extra tank in your boot and also mean you will never be able to take the car through the Channel Tunnel again, should that be a problem (on account of the potential for explosion). LPG offers cleaner emissions but slightly less fuel efficiency than petrol; and in terms of CO_2 performance it is on a par with petrol.

Not even a little bit green:

Almost any car that does a high mileage, lone occupant

It's not what you've got, it's how you use it. The mighty Bugatti Veyron, which kicks out an awesome 574 grams of CO_2 per kilometre thanks to its unspeakably powerful engine, should naturally belong here. But how many £840,000 Veyrons are actually going to go anywhere, apart from the short round trip from the Loews Hotel in Monte Carlo to the casino and back? Most will lurk in the controlled-atmosphere garages of the über-rich, to be unleashed only for the odd gambling excursion or brief 250 m.p.h. blast up the autobahn. The real un-green cars are simply any that do a big mileage each year. The corporate saloon that covers 20,000 miles a year with, say, a 40-mile-each-way commute will produce 6.4 tonnes of CO_2 (two-thirds of the national average carbon footprint) plus lots of all the other usual tailpipe nasties. The Veyron will need to do 11,000 miles to match that – and that's a lot of casino round trips. Finally, making sure just one person occupies a vehicle that can typically take five will really maximise its environmental impact.

MORE INFORMATION
G-Wiz electric car: www.goingreen.co.uk
Car-sharing schemes: www.carshare.com, www.liftshare.com,
www.citycarclub.co.uk
Official fuel economy and CO_2 statistics for all car models:
www.vcacarfueldata.org.uk
Information about conversions:
vegetable oil: www.dieselveg.com; LPG: www.lpga.co.uk

Chicken

(see also meat, p. 163; eggs, p. 104)

We have developed a fairly serious chicken habit in recent years, due at least in part to a perception that it is healthier than red meat. Our 20+ kilos per-person per-year consumption stacks up to about one chicken per week for a four-person household. To meet this demand, the British chicken industry kills 800 million birds a year, 98 per cent of them raised in intensive systems. The energy needed to raise the birds and produce their food amounts to over 4.5 TWh (billion kilowatt hours) per year, which is equivalent to the annual output of a decent coal-fired power station, or one per cent of the UK's electricity demands. And that's before we consider the energy used in processing, refrigeration, packaging and retailing. Intensive production, with its lower labour costs, has brought the price of a chicken down to a level that makes it affordable as a regular indulgence rather than the occasional treat of just a couple of decades ago. All this comes at significant cost to the chickens, which, along with pigs (see p. 204), have some of the most miserable lives of all farm animals. Counter-intuitively, in terms of energy use (and therefore CO_2 emissions) per bird, it is better for chickens to be miserable.

Deep green:
Chickens in the back yard

Try to raise your own chickens for meat sustainably and you will immediately become either (a) a chicken 'meat reducer' or (b) a fairly serious farmer. Keeping a couple of chickens for eggs (see p. 104) is one thing; having a flock for your own table is another, particularly if you plan to knock fifty-two of them on the head each year to feed an average family of four's chicken habit. To be truly green, chickens should eat no more than the food you grow for them; and their waste should be recycled on to your land. In order to keep your year's supply of birds well fed, you will therefore also need to be growing about two-thirds of an acre of a cereal crop such as wheat (which neatly illustrates the whole meat sustainability thing; see p. 163). If you choose to reduce your annual chicken-eating to well below average, then an edible flock becomes less of an issue. But there will still need to be cockerels, whose alarm-clock skills are rarely appreciated by neighbours, so backyard chicken breeding – deep green though it is – is best left to those in rural areas.

Dark green:
Conventional broiler chicken

Much has been written about the animal-welfare implications of breeding birds for ultra-rapid growth, cramming up to 40,000 of them into a windowless, dimly lit shed at a density of sixteen per square metre and having them shuffle around in their own excrement for their short and unpleasant forty-day lifespans. Look at chicken production purely in terms of energy use, though, and this system, bizarrely, has environmental advantages: the short lifespan, fast growth and crowded housing of over-bred, barn-reared chickens mean they use 32 per cent less energy per tonne of meat to rear than organic birds. So if greenhouse gases are your main worry, miserable intensive chickens get serious green points. On the environmental downside, their feed will itself have been intensively produced, and as 22 per cent of the feed is likely to be soya and 63 per cent of the world's soya is GM, then it is likely to have a GM component unless stated otherwise. Chicken production on this scale starts to produce very tangible levels of pollution: the average ammonia levels inside intensive broiler houses are above the safe level for humans. When the sheds are cleared after each 'crop' of chickens, powerful chemicals are needed to disinfect everything. Broiler litter has been described as 'the most toxic animal waste', but at least it is recycled: two-thirds of it goes on the land after having been composted and the remainder is burned in power stations. (So yes, one of your light bulbs is glowing courtesy of chicken shit.) There are 'nuances' within intensive chicken production. Assured Chicken Production (the red tractor logo) guarantees certain minimum welfare standards but still makes for a very intensive system. The RSPCA's 'Freedom Food' accreditation gives barn-reared birds a life that can be even better than in the worst free-range systems, but it's still an indoor life for a creature whose natural habitat is woodland. Given all of this, you may prefer to plump for a chicken that is less green in energy terms but has had a happier life and will almost certainly be better to eat.

Quite green:
Organic

Organic chickens use more energy and land than their intensively reared counterparts. But their feed, which accounts overall for 40 per cent of the energy cost of chicken production, is organic, which means it will not have been produced with fossil-fuel-based pesticides or energy-intensive artificial fertilizer. Such chickens live in small sheds of around 1,000 birds, rather than the megastructures that can contain flocks of up to 40,000 indoor chickens. They live twice as long as intensively reared birds, which of course means they need much more food, wherein lies their environmental downfall: but they can obtain some food naturally from their largely outdoor environment. The organic badge is not an absolute guarantee of the very best chicken you will eat: the one from the small producer at the farmers' market who can't afford to buy organic feed may well be tastier and just as sustainable. But with 'free range' (see below) often denoting little more than the presence of some holes in the walls of a shed packed with chickens, it means the chicken will have had fresh air, exercise and a good diet during its short life, all of which adds up to a better gastronomic and environmental experience.

Light green:
Free range

'Free range' sounds great but can in fact denote a fairly intensive method of chicken-rearing. Free-range birds must legally have access to the great outdoors for half of their 51-day life, where they must have 1 square metre of space each. Indoors, they are stocked at densities of thirteen birds per square metre. In practice, some of the free-range birds stuck in the middle of a big, closely packed shed may seldom see daylight. This doesn't necessarily make for the happiest chicken or the nicest roast, but the tight densities and short life will make for relatively low energy use.

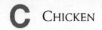

Pale green:
Traditional free range, free range 'total freedom'

Birds with these labels don't get an organic diet and they end up in bigger sheds of up to 4,000 birds. But they have the same lifespan as organic birds, continuous daylight, access to the outdoors from six weeks of age and a minimum outdoor space of 2 square metres each. 'Total freedom' birds additionally have unlimited outdoor space. In eating and welfare terms these birds are superior to free-range and conventional broilers: but with longer life, more space and non-organic feed they will have a high energy cost.

Not even a little bit green:
Processed chicken of uncertain provenance

Intensive chicken-farming is not particularly pleasant, but we do it more nicely here than elsewhere in the world. Chicken in ready meals, takeaways and processed food may well come from countries whose broiler sheds are worse than the UK's worst. This may not be an issue from an environmental-impact purist's point of view but it's a hard thought to ignore as you tuck in to your tikka masala. Such chicken may also have made a long, frozen journey from as far away as Brazil or Thailand and may also have been plumped up with water and proteins to, er, 'add value'.

Chocolate

*S*ometimes being green is about self-denial. Other times it is about changing behaviour. And in quite a few cases, especially where food is involved, it's about spending more money. Happily, in the case of chocolate, a bit of well-targeted extra expenditure brings you an infinitely superior product – one that has the added advantage of health benefits that do not normally accrue to food and drink products widely considered to be a vice. Like most high-value tropical crops, chocolate comes loaded with all sorts of environmental and ethical issues, from the use of slave labour (yes, today) on plantations to the clearing of 8 million hectares of richly biodiverse tropical forest (yes, an area four times the size of Wales). The other environmental issue is what, exactly, chocolate consists of: in many of the products we know and love as 'chocolate', cocoa solids and butter (which is what 'chocolate' really means) are only a minority ingredient amongst other, potentially ecologically destructive contents.

Deep green:
Fairtrade organic dark chocolate

You could give up chocolate as part of an overall personal 'save the planet' strategy. But a line has to be drawn somewhere. Doubtless there are many who would happily trade, say, an extra degree centigrade off the thermostat (which will have a much bigger effect on your carbon footprint; see p. 138) in order to retain a guilty pleasure like chocolate. As with most commodities, the main impact of chocolate is in its growing. Like coffee (see p. 75) it can grow as part of a sustainable 'agroforestry' system, underneath taller trees and amongst other crops. This limits the impact of its cultivation and reduces the need for chemical interventions. Although it is said to leave the smallest mark of all tropical cash crops, cocoa-growing is associated with forest clearance and the depletion of soils and bio-diversity. And with only 0.1 per cent of cocoa currently grown organically, it is fair to assume that agrochemicals will be used at some point in most cocoa production. So buying organic is the best guarantee that your chocolate will have been grown sustainably; choosing Fairtrade means that slave labour will not have been used and that the growers, mostly small farmers, will have received a guaranteed price for their crop.

Light green:
Dark chocolate with as much cocoa solids as possible

There are strong gastronomic and health reasons for choosing chocolate that advertises itself as being 60+ per cent cocoa solids. The good stuff tastes tremendous; plus it contains flavonoids and anti-oxidants that are thought to be jolly good for you and are said to be absent from milk or white chocolate. The chocolate from a non-organic/non-Fairtrade bar may have a dodgy provenance, but with all those cocoa solids, there's not much room for other ingredients. Vegetable oils feature highly in cheaper chocolate and may often be derived from palm oil, whose monocultural plantations are often established at the expense of rainforest. Sugar, too, is big in lesser chocolates and comes with its own environmental (and health) baggage (see p. 238).

Not particularly green:
Milk chocolate

It's a much guiltier pleasure than aristocratic 60 per cent cocoa solids dark chocolate for the simple reason that it contains more nonsense. Milk chocolate need only consist of 20 per cent cocoa solids and cocoa butter. Maybe 15 per cent will be milk solids (for more on milk, see p. 173), then much of the rest will be vegetable oil and sugar. Given that the oil could be palm oil, which is good neither for the environment nor, particularly, your health, and that we get through 222,000 tonnes of chocolate each year in Britain, most of which is not particularly green, then the smooth pleasure of milk chocolate loses out to its darker and stronger relatives.

Not even a little bit green:
Big boxes of chocs from 'big chocolate'

Four extremely large corporations control most of the world's chocolate market, doing what such corporations generally do: 'adding value' to a basic commodity so it can be sold at a healthy profit. Nothing malevolent about that, in pure economic terms: however, capitalism does have its unintended 'externalities'. Without any form of certification, there's no guarantee that your naughty box of chocs will have had sustainable origins or been produced without forced labour. And with all sorts of other ingredients and processing involved, plus vast amounts of seductive packaging, the giant box of chocs from a mainstream producer is easily the least green choice.

Clothing

Your choice of outfit may not make up anything like as big a chunk of your environmental footprint as your choice of car or central-heating boiler. But almost every aspect of clothing choice has an ecological impact. First, material. Cotton? Immense pesticide use and GM technology. Nylon? Derived from oil, polluting manufacturing process, doesn't biodegrade. Leather? Hungry livestock, nasty tanning processes. Wool? More hungry livestock, sheep dip. Then there's the choice of colour: white things, for example, come at a cost in terms of chemical bleaching and frequent hot washing. Washing clothes (see p. 267) accounts for 12 per cent of our water use and 10 per cent of domestic electricity use, never mind all the phosphates it chucks into our watercourses and the power used by tumble driers. In many cases, washing accounts for most of an item of clothing's environmental impact. And once you've tired of the garment, there's the issue of how to get rid of it: Britons each send 30 kilos of clothes to landfill each year, on average, with only a fraction recycled. Our clothes habit has been increasing rapidly, too, with the per-capita spend doubling since 1990 to about £650 per year, whilst the price of clothes has decreased relative to almost all other goods and services.

Deep green:
Second-hand, dark, slightly grubby, made from natural materials

As every student once knew (in the days before the £5 pair of jeans), charity shops provide a fine choice of perfectly serviceable clothing for very little money. Buying second-hand means no new materials or processes are needed; and you've just participated in the first and second 'Rs' (reduce and re-use) as well as encouraging someone to do the third (recycle) with their clothes. Dark clothes need the lowest-temperature washes; and limiting the amount of washing it gets is the single most important thing you can do to bring the shabby overcoat's eco-footprint near to zero. Finally, making sure your second-hand purchase is made of a natural material like wool or cotton will mean that when you've finally worn it to threads (which is, of course, what any deep greenie would do) it will biodegrade naturally, for example as mulch for something in the garden or a cover for the compost heap.

Dark green:
Clothes from sustainable materials

The problem with most clothes is that they are made from either fossil-fuel-derived synthetic fabrics (see below) or natural crops with a heavy environmental cost (see cotton, p. 70). Help is at hand from a growing range of clothes derived from crops which are grown organically or can be grown in a low-impact manner. Hemp is a productive, easy-to-grow, pest-tolerant crop that makes durable, breathable fabrics. Despite its feeble concentrations of the psycho-active ingredient tetrahydrocannabinol, hemp production has been banned in many countries (notably the USA) for many years because it is a strain of *Cannabis sativa*. However, hemp is now grown in the UK and hemp-based clothing is increasingly available. Flax, the basis of linen, is a similarly tough crop; and even fast-growing bamboo can be turned into clothes. Organic cottons will have a higher impact and more clothes miles (as cotton is a subtropical crop) but at least they will be free of cotton's major environmental impact. And low-impact materials don't all have to be scratchy: silk gets sustainability points as it encourages the planting of many white mulberry trees, on whose leaves the silkworms responsible for most of the world's silk exclusively feed. Wool is relatively sustainable, given the low-impact nature of much sheep farming; organic sheep farming is even less energy-intensive. Finally, recycled polyester clothing (such as fleeces made from drinks bottles) is available; however, there is still a problem with final disposal of such materials. It goes without saying that, to stay dark green, clothes from sustainable materials should be minimally washed, then either handed on or recycled when they are no longer wanted.

Pale green:
Clothes made from farmed or wild animal hides

Whether it's farmed cattle, cute furry animals or endangered Tibetan antelopes, clothes made from animals that must die to provide them have been the subject of vehement protest for some time. But through the prism of pure environmentalism, they don't merit quite the same degree of demonization. Sure, where species (and therefore precious biodiversity) are endangered, it's a big environmental deal. But if it's possible to farm (or hunt) animals for their hides sustainably, then on the grounds that the end product could be a low-impact, renewable material, it doesn't quite end up in the eco-doghouse. Squirrel-skin gloves (grey, of course) anyone?

Not particularly green:
White cotton everything

Cotton, the world's most important non-food agricultural crop, accounts for over 20 per cent of the world's pesticide usage; many of these pesticides feature in the World Health Organization's 1a, 'Extremely hazardous', classification; and many are applied by unprotected developing-country agricultural workers, of whom 20,000 die of pesticide poisoning each year. To get round the pesticide problem, GM strains have been introduced which secrete a toxin that poisons the bollworm, cotton's major pest. Around one third of global cotton production is now GM; and whilst this cuts pesticide use by up to 70 per cent, a Cornell University study of Chinese growers showed that, after several years, a rise in other pests that were previously kept down by the spray and the bollworms led to a return to pre-GM levels of spraying. Cotton is also a major guzzler of irrigation water, and is the crop largely responsible for the near-disappearance of the Aral Sea. So, as a material, cotton has its issues, to say the least. Everything white means lots of hot washing, which cranks up cotton clothing's impact yet further.

Not even a little bit green:
Fossil-fuel-derived artificial fabrics, lots of dry-cleaning

Cotton may be an ecological disaster area but at least it is renewable and biodegradable. Fabrics such as nylon and polyester are derived from oil and manufactured in industrial processes that are energy- and water-intensive and chuck out all sorts of emissions. And to add insult to ecological injury, such fabrics are neither biodegradable nor compostable, and thus hang around for years in landfill or add further to air pollution if they are incinerated. To get your clothes' eco-footprint as big as possible, lots of dry cleaning (see p. 270) will be the icing on the cake.

Cod

Poor old cod. Fished virtually out of existence on the Grand Banks off Newfoundland, where it was once so abundant it was said to impede the progress of explorers' boats. And fished to the brink of extinction elsewhere, especially in the North Sea, where the remaining 'spawning biomass' is at a level considered to be one third of the bare minimum. The International Council for the Exploration of the Seas (ICES) has called for a complete ban on fishing here and in the Irish Sea and off the west of Scotland to allow stocks to recover; but shutting down the cod fishery is beyond the will of most politicians. Britain consumes one third of the world's cod stocks, mainly in the form of fish and chips: can our trips to the chippy ever be green?

Deep green:
No cod

Even the greenest forms of cod (see p. 73) carry some environmental cost. Indeed it's difficult to find any fish that doesn't have some issues (see fish, p. 114). Better to leave the over-fished cod to its long, natural lifespan and choose a local species that is being fished within sustainable levels. A link to lists of sustainable fish is given on p. 74.

Dark green:
MSC-certified Pacific cod

The Marine Stewardship Council awards its certification to fisheries that are managed sustainably. It was originally established by Unilever, which may raise some anti-corporate hackles; but it is surely in the long-term interest of any sensible seller of fish products to secure a long-term future for its raw materials. The Pacific cod fishery uses long-line fishing, which avoids the seabed destruction caused by trawling but risks creating 'bird by-catch'. However, the Pacific cod fishery is assessed regularly for the impact of by-catch and can be closed if acceptable levels are exceeded. There may be over 4,000 food miles involved in Pacific cod, but these are by sea rather than air as the fish is frozen immediately after it is caught.

Quite green:
Icelandic or Faroese cod

ICES thinks that cod-fishing in these waters should be scaled down, but these fisheries are the nearest ones to the UK that are not in imminent danger of collapse. There has been a gentle decline in catch in the last five years, but Iceland in particular has a profound vested interest in maintaining its cod stocks, which are by far the most important fish export in a country for whom fish exports are a very big deal. Icelandic cod is, however, caught mostly by bottom trawling, which damages the seabed.

Not particularly green:
Organic farmed cod

Cod farming is a response to crashing wild populations. Its proponents argue that it is free from some of the problems of salmon farming: for example, because cod are non-migratory, their behaviour is less disrupted by being kept in a pen. Organic cod farming uses no chemicals, growth promoters or anti-fouling agents, and the fish are not susceptible to the sea lice that plague farmed salmon. They are also fed on the offcuts from wild fish, so other creatures are not caught or farmed specifically to feed them. However, farmed cod do need to be dosed with an antibiotic to protect against a common disease. And as the industry is still young, it is still possible that it may turn out to have the negative environmental impacts of other types of aquaculture – for example, farmed fish escaping and weakening the wild stock through interbreeding.

Not even a little bit green:
Any old cod

Choose cod without care and the chances are it will have come from a crashing fishery somewhere in the world. Much cod eaten in Britain comes from the North Sea, Barents Sea and the waters around Norway, all of whose stocks are in steep – some say terminal – decline.

MORE INFORMATION
Marine Conservation Society website with information on sustainable fish: www.fishonline.org

Coffee

*P*ut your environmentalist's hat on and conjure up an image of tropical cash crops and what springs to mind? Vast, chemically managed monocultures owned by big conglomerates and providing harsh, poorly paid conditions for a few workers? Coffee subverts this picture. For a start, it is an evergreen crop which keeps fruiting for up to twenty years, meaning that land does not have to be constantly dug up and replanted. It can grow in the shade of a larger forest, so there is no need for clear-cutting with its devastating impact on biodiversity. Around 70 per cent of the world's coffee is grown on small farms, directly supporting 20 million farmers for whom the crop is their only livelihood. So turning your nose up at coffee in the name of the environment may not be a good move: the chances are that less lucrative and therefore more extensive and damaging crops would ultimately be planted in its place. More and more coffee is grown in intensive monocultures: but with many different labelling schemes it is possible to avoid this and make positive coffee choices.

Deep green:
Fairtrade, organic, shade-grown coffee

Often the deepest green option involves self-denial: not in this case. Sustainably grown coffee is one of the lowest-impact forms of agriculture available. Because the plants are perennial they help to stabilize and build soils, preventing runoff and soil erosion. And thanks to the ability of certain varieties to grow as the 'understorey' of a rainforest, coffee production can be that rarest of things:

agriculture that preserves and promotes biodiversity. Such shade-grown situations encourage many bird species, whose appetite for bugs largely obviates the need for pesticides. There are several certification schemes for coffee, none of which is entirely without problems or beyond criticism. Fairtrade offers a guaranteed minimum price for producers and most coffee so badged is shade-grown. Organic coffee is grown without artificial fertilizer or pesticides and is mostly grown with some form of shade. Rainforest Alliance coffee is grown to standards aimed at protecting ecosystems but does allow limited use of agrochemicals.

Dark green:
Dandelion-root coffee

Hardcore greenies who have taken the 'eat local' mantra to its logical extreme must forgo the joys of fine shade-grown coffee. They must also eschew weird coffee substitutes, some of whose ingredients do not grow in temperate climes. For them, dandelion-coffee awaits. It's dark green because dandelions are abundant; those harvesting them for coffee will be very popular with many gardeners. It's caffeine-free, sadly, but said to have health-giving properties.

Pale green:
Uncertified coffee of indeterminate provenance

Although most coffee is grown on a small scale, when it isn't shade-grown, organic or Fairtrade, it could be from large monoculture plantations which can be on cleared rainforest, support little bio-diversity and demand the use of agrochemicals.

Not particularly green:
Instant coffee

In most of the world, instant coffee accounts for around 20 per cent of all coffee drunk. In the UK, it's 80 per cent. What's wrong with us? A perfectly decent product, wrested from the jungle by honest, hard-working peasants (very possibly in a sustainable manner), is then mucked about with in a series of energy-intensive industrial processes to produce an inferior product. Soluble coffee is obtained by extracting the coffee's 'essence' in much the same way a percolator does, then concentrating this essence and either spray- or freeze-drying it. Gastronomic and environmental madness.

Not even a little bit green:
Decaffeinated instant coffee

To add insult to injury, why not remove the only worthwhile ingredient from a by now entirely denatured product, and in doing so increase its environmental impact still further? (See also tea, p. 241.)

Compost and fertilizer

*W*ow. *There are shades of green for compost and fertilizer? Isn't all gardening green? Not quite. The world of keeping your garden growing is fraught with eco-peril. It's a simple problem: you need to 'top up' the soil's fertility on a regular basis because many of the things we like to grow, particularly fruit and vegetables, remove nutrients from the soil to power their growth. Not all the methods of putting back these nutrients are ecologically benign. Artificial fertilizer, for example, is produced in a highly energy-intensive industrial process. Much commercially sold compost is extracted from peat bogs, delicate ecosystems that do not recover from being strip-mined to keep our back gardens healthy. Happily, there are green ways to make your garden grow; and the very greenest methods are also the easiest and cheapest.*

Deep green:
Your own compost and manure

Making your own compost surrounds you with an aura of ecological righteousness that extends way beyond the fact that it is the lowest-impact way of adding fertility to your soil. A simple 'cold' compost heap (one that takes about a year to produce usable material) will deal with all of your fruit and veg peelings and waste as well as much of your garden rubbish and any newspaper or cardboard you have lying around. If you eat your greens and read a lot, that's a serious weight of rubbish that would otherwise be sent to landfill, where it would decay anaerobically and produce methane, a potent greenhouse gas.

For an average household, composting can equate to saving a quarter of a tonne of CO_2 per year. Your compost heap can also take part in the household's water-saving activities as a recipient for that fine compost activator: human urine (see p. 253). The end result is a free, high-quality soil improver. If you have a small garden then you will probably be able to make all the compost you will ever need; as gardens and veg-growing operations expand, though, you will need to 'import' fertility (see below). If you have a composting toilet (see p. 251) its results can be used around fruit trees and bushes; and if you keep other livestock, such as hens (see p. 60), their offerings will make the garden very happy indeed.

Dark green:
Something else's manure, preferably organic

The output of herbivorous livestock makes a superb soil improver and fertilizer, provided it has been left to rot down for a while. The intense hit of fertility that it provides will mean that you only need to 'muck' the garden once every three years or so. Because of the volumes that even a small garden will need, buying well-rotted animal manure from garden centres is a ludicrously expensive business; however, depending on where you live, it can be obtained for little or no money from stables and farms. Horse manure is the gold standard but cow, pig and chicken manures all provide fine service too. Getting manure from organic, or at least small-scale, farms lessens the chance of feed additives getting into your own food chain.

Quite green:
Peat-free compost

Peat (see below) has serious environmental issues. If you don't need vast quantities of soil improver, or need a medium for growing things from seed or potting, then peat-free compost is the next best option. Many retailers stock peat-free varieties which are based on composted bark, green waste or coir. The latter comes from tropical latitudes but is shipped in large volumes to reduce its compost miles per cubic metre. If you can't do without peat then there is a variety of compost made from filtered moorland water, which means peat is extracted with no impact on the fragile moorland itself.

Not particularly green:
Peat-based compost

Peat makes fantastic compost: it adds nutrients to soil, improves its structure and increases its capacity to retain water. The problem with peat is that it is extracted from bog ecosystems that are rich wildlife habitats and regenerate only very slowly, at the rate of as little as one millimetre per year. Vigorous environmental campaigning has restricted peat extraction in the UK, which means that peat-based composts now mostly threaten someone else's ecosystems. Most peat imported into this country for gardening purposes comes from Estonia and from Latvia, where peat extraction is the country's fourth-biggest industry. However, with many UK retailers going peat-free and the Peat Producers' Association having renamed itself the Growing Media Association, the writing seems to be on the wall for peat as a back-garden soil improver. Still, if its absence isn't specifically stated on the pack, assume that the compost has peat in it.

Not even a little bit green:
Inorganic nitrogen fertilizer

Heavily used in agriculture but also available for gardeners, these fertilizers will offer a 'quick fix' of NPK (nitrogen, phosphorus and potassium) to your garden but, unlike the other options discussed here, won't contribute to building your soil structure if used alone. Much nitrogen fertilizer is synthesized from atmospheric nitrogen in a process that consumes one per cent of the entire world energy supply.

Computers

Now here's a complex subject. On the one hand, computers are terribly ungreen. They can be full of nasty substances and the constant upgrade cycle — in which your spanking new state-of-the-art machine is revealed as yesterday's news about, ooh, two weeks after you buy it — creates mountains of waste. And, of course, computers are deeply fond of electricity. On the other hand, they can save resources by removing the need for physical items to be shuffled about the place: think digital music, documents, working from home, even online shopping, which potentially reduces car journeys. But then along comes the revelation that — thanks to the many powerful computers involved — an avatar (player's online character) in virtual world *Second Life* might consume as much electricity as a real-world resident of Brazil. No straightforward answers, then: but some shades of green can always be discerned.

Deep green:
Grumpy Luddite

The very greenest way to compute is not to compute at all. The UK's casual domestic web-surfing alone accounts, at a conservative estimate, for a stonking 1.52TWh (billion kilowatt hours) per year, the output of a small-scale hydroelectricity plant. And that's just the home PCs, never mind all the data centres, server farms, etc., that are also needed to keep the digital world turning. If you're living a seriously deep green lifestyle then — in the event that you have been so decadent as to have electricity — you'll be using it for serious stuff like charging power tools and lighting the workshop, not fossicking around on that intraweb thingy.

Dark green:
Slightly less grumpy Luddite who goes to the odd Internet café from time to time

Even the frugal, electricity-free Amish (see also p. 109) permit themselves to use computers at an outside workplace. This must surely prove that computers have finally become genuinely indispensable. But with almost everything you can usefully do on a computer, from email to word processing, now available as a web-based application, who needs their own? A few borrowed moments on someone else's machine, or a cheap hour in the library or the local Internet caff, will do the trick. You're free from the constant pressure to upgrade your hardware, from 'Gates' Law' (in which software seems gradually to slow down, compelling you to upgrade the hardware too) and from all the nasties that are still involved in building and disposing of a new machine.

Quite green:
Laptop

Since they stopped looking like briefcases, laptops have consistently been cool. They get green points for consuming, at around 30W, one third of the power of a desktop machine; and, of course, they don't need separate monitors, which crank up most desktops' consumption even further (see below). You could even hijack someone else's wireless Internet signal, although with an Internet router using only around 10W, doing so isn't going to make a massive dent in your carbon footprint and may brass off your neighbour. Choose your manufacturer with care, though: Greenpeace's *Green Electronics* guide ranks electronics manufacturers according to their use of harmful chemicals (such as PVC and brominated flame retardants) and their recycling policies. At the time of writing – and perhaps surprisingly – Apple, purveyor of the world's coolest laptops, is at the bottom of the list. Laptops are also relatively frugal in standby mode, using a shade under 3W on average, but it's always greenest to switch them off. To be hyper-green, very light exercise on a modified exercise bike (or a real bike hooked up to a generator) will easily run a laptop and make using your computer a less sedentary experience.

Pale green:

Desktop with a smallish LCD monitor, staying away from virtual communities

Desktop machines usually provide more processing oomph than laptops for less money, which is great; but this inevitably means more juice is required. They use around 90W on average, about three times the power of an average laptop. But their monitors need power, too: from around 40W for an LCD to 90W for a CRT (cathode ray, 'old fashioned') monitor and off into the wattage stratosphere for plasma screens (see below). So, assuming one survey's claimed average Internet use of 3.5 hours per day, your desktop usage, though not expensive in electricity terms, could still release 70kg of CO_2 into the atmosphere each year, the equivalent of a sedate drive from London to Manchester. Still, staying away from watt-hungry virtual worlds might help to reduce your impact on the real one. And you might also like to stay away from those distributed programs like SETI@home, which borrow a bit of your computer's processing power to do stuff like search for extraterrestrial life: by increasing its usage they will also boost its power demands and, ultimately, your electricity bill.

Not even a little bit green:
Monster-gaming PC hooked up to giant plasma screen

Serious PC gamers boast that their rooms don't need heating: their mighty PCs do it for them. The laws of computing not yet having slipped free of the laws of physics, the more you want to do with your computer, the more power you need. And modern computer games place big demands on processing power. High-end gaming models come with 1kW power supplies and the most beastly ones need liquid cooling to tame their torrid chips. Stick on a big plasma screen for a completely immersive gaming experience, and a serious habit could have you achieving a third of a UK household's annual electricity consumption from gaming alone. Consoles use less power, but with the Xbox said to draw up to 160W and the PlayStation 3 suspected to need even more, they're not entirely frugal. Eco-gamers (if such people exist) are pointed at the Nintendo Wii, currently the most frugal of the top consoles.

MORE INFORMATION
Green computing guide, via Greenpeace: www.greenpeace.org

Cookers

The greenness of your cooking depends much more on the food you buy than on what you cook it with. Even a raw-food diet will be contributing to planetary catastrophe if its ingredients are air-freighted, slathered in chemicals and trussed up in poncy packaging. Still, you can make a difference with your choice of cooker, which accounts for about 2 per cent of total household energy use and around 8 per cent of your electricity bill.

Deep green:
Raw-food diet

Now there's a seriously green choice, if ever there was one. Not only will failing to cook help to make your diet carbon-neutral by saving 2 per cent of your household energy footprint, it will also do you a power of good: fruit and veg in particular are much better for you in their raw state. No cooking also means plenty of time for anything from meditation to computer gaming, depending where you fit elsewhere on the sustainable scale. And that cooker-shaped gap in your kitchen could become something really green and groovy, like a zero-power fridge (see p. 122), a wormery or just somewhere to keep all that dried algae you will need to be eating. Clearly this rather radical approach creates problems for lovers of pork, chicken and some fish and shellfish: but there's still steak tartare, sashimi and a host of other uncooked, dried and preserved surf 'n' turf options for those of us who want to go raw without going veggie. It goes without saying that, for maximum eco-friendliness, everything should be chopped, peeled, juiced, etc., by hand. No cheating with food processors, eh?

Dark green:
Induction hob plus gas oven

From no-tech to high-tech: induction hobs use the least energy of all cooking methods, operating at 84 per cent efficiency compared to 40 per cent for gas. The reason for this is that the heat is applied directly to the food: the pan gets hot but the hob doesn't, bizarrely, thanks to electromagnetic magic. The only drawbacks are cost – still high but coming down – and the fact that induction hobs don't work with aluminium, glass and most stainless-steel cookware. There's no such thing as an induction oven, though, so natural gas is the best option for baking and roasting beneath your spiffy induction hob, being the lowest-CO_2 fossil-fuel option (see below for why).

Quite green:
Wood stove

This has the advantage of being completely carbon-neutral and renewable. But sadly, for those attracted by the evocative smell of wood smoke, the homely allure of warm cast iron and the general feeling of ecological self-righteousness, there are some serious drawbacks with wood-burning. Wood-fired ranges are not cheap (being in the two-grand-plus price bracket), most will be illegal to use in Smoke Control Zones (which is most urban areas) and then there's the question of where you are going to get and keep the several tons of (sustainably sourced) wood you will need each year. And that's before you start to worry about keeping the blasted thing alight all day or the fact that you are chucking nasty pollutants into the atmosphere. And another thing: if we all cooked this way, an area of land ten times the size of the UK would have to be given over to coppiced woodland. Still, you could run your central heating off a wood-burning cooker, which is one advantage . . .

Light green:
Natural gas hob and oven

Burning fossil fuels is never a particularly green thing to do, but cooking with gas kicks out a great deal less CO_2 than cooking with electricity, because the latter has had to be generated (mostly by fossil fuels, in this country), then transported to your home via the grid (see electricity, p. 109). Gas hobs are much less efficient than electric ones in transferring heat to pans, but the conversion losses from electricity generation cancel this out. There are as yet no energy ratings for gas cookers that help you to make the greenest choice, but there are plans to introduce these by 2008. What with gas being more controllable than electricity, this is the 'least worst' choice if you are connected to mains gas.

Not particularly green:
Electric cookers

Because – as described above – electricity is a 'secondary' energy source, it's always going to be a bigger kicker-out of CO_2 than the relatively clean natural gas. Plus there's the fact that the poor controllability of old-style electric rings and hobs means that more energy is wasted during cooking, even if the rings themselves are 60–75 per cent efficient. The greenest electrical cooking combo is a halogen hob (which offers instant heat and better controllability) and a fan oven, which uses 20 per cent less electricity than a conventional electric oven. Electric ovens have energy ratings (from A for the best to G for the worst) to help you choose.

Not even a little bit green:
Fossil-fuel-fired cast-iron range

OK, so they may be made of recycled iron and heavy with cosy rural symbolism, but cast-iron ranges are a bit of an ecological nightmare once you run them on fossil fuels. That they are hot all the time is part of their charm and also their biggest problem: cooking accounts for less than 5 per cent of a range's fuel use. Run a two-oven Aga on kerosene or diesel and it will get through 40 litres a week, which is the equivalent of driving 65 miles a day in an economical car. Run one on electricity and it will use at least twice as much as cooking normally does. You can run hot water and sometimes central heating off them, which helps (but which also cranks up their fuel consumption); however, there are much more efficient ways of doing this.

Not even a little bit green 2:
Microwaves

It is unfair and entirely subjective thus to condemn microwaves. They use up to 70 per cent less electricity than conventional ovens and are small and space-efficient. But as they are mainly used to reheat ready meals that are full of rubbish and should have been cooked from scratch in the first place, or to defrost food that would have been better fresh, they have no place in an eco-friendly – or indeed a civilized – kitchen.

MORE INFORMATION
Background information from the Energy Saving Trust:
www.est.org.uk

Courgettes

*D*espite having a very short history in this country's diet (apart from in its larger form as a marrow), the courgette has shot to prominence in recent years. Our courgette imports doubled from 1995 to 2005 and it now ranks as Britain's tenth favourite vegetable. All of this popularity carries an environmental cost: we expect courgettes to be on the table all year round, when their natural outdoor season in this country is confined to the summer months. So imports from as far away as southern Africa fill the seasonal gap. How green is your courgette? It's all in the timing.

Deep green:
No courgettes

Where food-growing is concerned, the ultra-purist deep greenie is interested in the nutritional bang you get for your environmental buck. In the case of courgettes, it's not a very loud one. Apart from their seeds, courgettes contain little nutritional value, are bulky to transport, perish quickly and have a limited season. Far better to concentrate your growing (or shopping) efforts on something more worthy and nutritious.

Dark green:
Your own courgettes; lots of chutney for the rest of the year

Few of us would, however, be prepared to consider courgette absti-nence as part of a practical planet-saving strategy. Growing your own takes little effort and few inputs, apart from a bit of water and compost. It can be space-intensive, though: a single courgette plant can completely take over a small vegetable bed. And the problem is that the plants tend to produce a glut in a short period of time, so if you want to extend the courgette experience, the only option is preservation, which with courgettes means chutney. In green terms, chutney probably loses out to eating imported out-of-season cour-gettes, on account of all the energy-intensive cooking and extra ingredients it needs, but hey . . . it's fun to make and much better to eat.

Quite green:
Local courgettes in summer

The season for locally grown British courgettes runs from June to September: the earliest ones may have been grown under cover; later courgettes are more likely to have led a completely outdoor life. Eating courgettes in season minimizes food miles and gives you a better chance of a good eating experience, because courgettes don't keep or travel particularly well. As to organics versus conventional: courgettes get relatively low dosages of pesticides, around one spray each of herbicide, insecticide and fungicide. As a result, only 4 per cent of samples recently tested had residues; however, many of these were of dieldrin, an insecticide that was banned in 1981 but is still widely present in the environment and thought to be picked up by courgettes' deep roots in dry weather.

Pale green:

Organic European imports in spring and autumn

Go beyond our shores for your courgettes and the food miles – mainly by road from southern Europe – rack up. Choosing organic imports might offset this a little, as no energy will have been needed to create the agrochemicals that conventional courgettes need.

Not even a little bit green:

Air-freighted courgettes in the depths of winter

If we are to take the view that air-freighting food is generally an environmentally problematic idea (see also pp. 32 and 129 for discussion of the issues), then air-freighting a vegetable that contains mainly water and little in the way of nutrition is seriously problematic. Courgettes from Africa in the depths of winter are a daft idea, particularly when there's so much that's fresh, green and a great deal more nutritious closer to home.

Courgette season

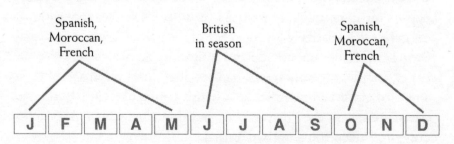

Spanish, Moroccan, French

British in season

Spanish, Moroccan, French

| J | F | M | A | M | J | J | A | S | O | N | D |

Dairy products: cheese, butter, cream, yoghurt

The impact of dairy products on the environment is of course intimately tied to milk (see p. 173). Thanks to the hunger and the digestive habits of cattle, dairy practised on an industrial scale makes a significant contribution to global warming and the pollution of ecosystems. But on a small-farm or smallholding scale, dairy cattle are pivotal figures. They provide valuable food products, by-products of which can be 'recycled' into the enterprise (as in the great Parmesan cheese/Parma ham symbiosis in which pigs feed on the whey from the cheese-making process), and superb fertilizer, all as a result of having grazed on natural pasture and forage. So the greenness of your dairy choices depends mainly on the extent to which the cheese, cream, butter or yoghurt was produced in a sustainable manner.

Deep green:
Light consumption of local, artisanal, unpasteurized stuff

As with all animal products in the human food supply, abstinence is the lowest-impact choice. But renouncing dairy products can be a tough business for non-vegans. If you can't face a future of margarine or cheese based on soya protein, there are plenty of ways to make sure your dairy choices tread lightly on the Earth. And there is an

93

argument that the existence of small-scale dairy makes a positive contribution by providing fertilizer that enables more efficient use of land. Local, artisanal cheese will almost inevitably have been made with milk from a small-scale operation that may not be organic but will certainly be far from industrial. And if the dairy product is unpasteurized then there will be even less energy involved in production. There will be minimal food miles involved and you'll be voting, financially, for more of the same, which will stimulate the growing market for distinctive local produce.

Dark green:
Artisanal stuff from not too far away, organics from the UK

We are largely self-sufficient in milk in this country, yet we import about as much cheese as we produce. Being only 21 miles away from the greatest cheese-producing nation on earth has something to do with this. Many French cheeses are, like many of ours, produced in industrial systems but many are also highly distinctive, with protected status and rigorously controlled production standards. Eating these is a vote for agricultural diversity as well as a great idea from a purely gastronomic point of view. Organic cream, butter and yoghurt are all widely available in supermarkets and derive from agriculture that has a (relatively) low environmental impact.

Not even a little bit green:

Believing all the ludicrous scaremongering hype about the evils of dairy products and eating margarine, artificial cream in aerosol tins, lurid low-fat yoghurt in many tiny pots, etc.

Sometimes (albeit rarely) trying to be healthy is the least green option. The world of 'healthy' dairy alternatives is largely predicated on the idea that all dairy products are inherently bad for you, particularly in terms of fat consumption. As with virtually any food, too much dairy is a bad thing. But the fats in good dairy products such as butter can promote, rather than damage, health. The synthetic trans-fats in refined vegetable-oil products such as margarines can, however, have the opposite effect. And the term 'vegetable oil' might mean palm oil, whose plantations often spread at the expense of virgin rainforest. Even if it is a more locally grown plant oil (sunflower, say, or rapeseed), its production will most likely have taken place in a highly industrialized monoculture. Aerosol-powered artificial cream, with its ludicrous overpackaging and unspecified hydrogenated vegetable oil, must surely be one of the most environmentally damaging ways to avoid dairy. At least the cans can be recycled, though, unlike yoghurt pots, whose polystyrene packaging is not currently a class of plastic that can be easily turned into other things and so most go to landfill or incineration. Removing the already low levels of fat from yoghurt can take away the vitamins you need to absorb its calcium goodness; and the various natural and artificial sweeteners many such products contain aren't really helping either your health or the environment.

Drinking water

Worrying about the greenness of the water we drink is, on the face of it, pretty decadent, given that one in six people worldwide does not have access to clean drinking water. Still, seeing as we've got it, we might as well go on to make sure it is as eco-friendly as possible. The question wouldn't have arisen a few years ago: clean drinking water is one of the things we simultaneously took for granted but also valued enormously. Since the large-scale arrival of fancy bottled water on these shores, though, we've been moved to question whether 'corporation pop' is really the best thing to drink. Look at the subject through the prism of sustainability as well as health, though, and some clear 'shades' emerge.

Deep green:
Your own spring

Pure drinking water from a clean stream or groundwater source is by far the greenest option, albeit one available only to a tiny minority. As long as you need minimal infrastructure to set up your supply and the water is delivered by gravity or a renewable-energy device such as a ram pump (which uses the power of water flow to pump it up hill), or maybe a solar-/wind-powered pump, then it will be as eco-friendly as water supply can get. Whether it's as good for you as tap water is a moot point, though: for example, if the nearby farmer is regularly soaking the surrounding fields with pesticides, you'd be better off with mains water from a health point of view.

Dark green:
Tap water

The water industry uses 6,000GWh per year, which is about the output of a single coal-fired power station (or the UK's total hydro-electric-generating capacity). It builds dams, uses many chemicals and in some areas controversially dumps fluoride in the water supply. But the end result is the miracle of clean water, which passes extremely rigorous quality standards in 99.74 per cent of UK cases, being piped to almost every home that needs it. Tap water has frequently beaten bottled water in taste tests and, unlike some bottled waters, does not have a mineral content that can make it dangerous to feed to infants. And to put the energy use into context, it takes 94kWh a year to supply the average family with the 200 cubic metres they use per year, which is about the same as three appliances left on standby.

Quite green:
Purified rainwater

If you have a thing about tap water despite the evidence, there's a potential supply of drinking water on your roof (see also water (supply), p. 276). Very few houses catch 200m³ per year, though: the average is more like 50m³. So radical water-conservation measures are needed to get your water use down to a level where there will be enough drinking water left over per person (5 litres per day to allow for lots of exercise). It should also be pointed out that water used for bathing and washing should be of drinking quality. Despite its pristine image, rainwater shares the same category as sewage in the eyes of the law, because it may have been contaminated on your roof by bird or rodent faeces. The most reliable way to purify it is to filter it then apply ultraviolet light. This destroys the DNA (sunbed users take note) of the offending micro-organisms. With an always-on 55W bulb that will also need annual replacement, this process will consume 480kWh per year, over a tenth of the average household electricity consumption, and five times the energy the water company uses to do the same job.

Not particularly green:
Local 'natural mineral water' in a glass bottle

Rosy-cheeked perfect human specimens have been leaping around in commercials for years to convince us that mineral water is to be associated with purity in all its forms. Of late, the environmental movement has been jumping about with equal vigour to point out it is ecologically insane to extract, bottle and transport a resource to homes which have a perfectly good alternative available at the twist of a tap. The World Health Organization is 'unaware of any convincing evidence to support the beneficial effects of consuming such mineral waters'. Leaving aside this, and the fact that mineral water costs around 500 times more than tap water per litre, the environmental costs are not inconsiderable. The polyethylene terephthalate (PET) bottles in which much water is bottled take 1.5 billion barrels of oil annually just to make. In the UK, only 14 per cent of local authorities can recycle plastics; and 50 per cent of our plastics are shipped to China for recycling. The majority of plastic mineral water bottles that make it to landfill take hundreds of years to biodegrade. Our imports and transportation of mineral water are estimated to result in the emission of 33,000 tonnes of CO_2 annually. All a bit daft, really, in a world of finite mineral resources and climate change. If you want to drink mineral water, the category 'natural mineral water' is the most rigorously checked; local sourcing will minimize the drink miles and glass bottles are not oil-based, indefinitely recyclable and more widely recycled.

Not even a little bit green:
Mineral water in a plastic bottle, from far, far away

The next grades down of mineral water are 'spring water', which must have come from a single, non-polluted groundwater source, but can have been treated; and 'table water', which can come from any one source, including the public water supply. Anyone doubting that drinks companies have an occasional penchant for cynicism should remember the UK fiasco of Dasani, Coca-Cola's bottled tap water whose treatment process introduced potentially carcinogenic bromate into the product. However, for maximum environmental damage from a mineral water, distance is the key. Current frontrunner in these stakes must be Fiji water, whose very remoteness is its selling point. No calculations are necessary to work out that importing water 10,000 miles to a country not normally known for its overall absence of the commodity is not environmentally sensible. Add an oil-based un-biodegradable plastic bottle (that may also leach minute quantities of antimony into the product) for maximum environmental impact.

Drugs (illegal)

*M*uch is known of the risks to health, lifestyle and liberty that illegal drugs present. But what about the ecological issues? Anyone with a serious habit is hardly likely to be quizzing their dealer earnestly about whether the wrap of cocaine they are about to score is fair trade or organic. But whether the Home Office likes it or not, people take drugs: and in a world where every purchasing decision has important environmental nuances, maybe there should be greater awareness of the shades of green involved.

Deep green:

Magic mushrooms

Gone are the days when one could innocently pick psychoactive fungi and lie around watching the purple turkeys flap languidly overhead without fear of legal consequence. 'Magic mushrooms' – those which contain similar hallucinogenic ingredients to LSD – are now up in the 'most harmful' class A, where mere possession can land you with a seven-year stretch in chokey. In environmental terms, though, wild mushrooms are seasonal, local and in most cases probably organic, giving them the lightest possible ecological footprint.

Dark green:
Cannabis, grown locally outdoors

The ethical and environmental consequences of the international drugs trade are nasty in the extreme (see heroin, cocaine, below). Local, illegal horticulture cuts out the drug miles and, to an extent, the warlords and geopolitical issues. But it can also be a bit of an energy vampire if the growing techniques are too high-tech. Strains of the plant that are suited to a temperate climate can grow quite happily outdoors, with no need for heat and light or for chemical fertilizers and pesticides; and processing the plants is a chemical-free, low-energy affair.

Pale green:
Cannabis, grown locally indoors

Indoor growing soon turns cannabis cultivation from an environmentally benign pursuit into something a lot more power-hungry. To replicate the long hours of full-spectrum daylight preferred by the highest-yielding strains, a lot of electricity-guzzling high-pressure sodium and metal halide lamps are used. The temperature needs to be controlled; fans and extractors are needed to keep the plants happy and vent off suspicious odours; and much reflective material – none of which is even vaguely compostable or renewable – is needed. Unless the indoor grower is using a reputable green-tariff electricity supplier (see p. 111), the substantial power demands of this technique alone make it distinctly unsustainable.

Not particularly green:
Ecstasy, LSD, manufactured locally

Because they can be synthesized locally by people skilled in chemistry, these two, like cannabis, can largely avoid the drug miles issues. But given that chemical manufacturing processes – particularly illegal ones – are rarely green, they end up towards the bottom of the list.

Not green at all:
Heroin

It may derive from a plant, and may also support the economy of at least one impoverished nation state. But this doesn't make heroin in any way green. The refinement of opium into heroin involves nasty, toxic chemicals. And its phenomenal value (Afghan heroin, estimated to account for 87 per cent of global production, has a final worth of nearly $200 billion) fosters international organized crime networks whose members are not generally known for their commitment to green issues.

Not even a little bit green:
Cocaine

Nothing could be further from fair trade or organic than good old Charlie. Leaving aside all the serious humanitarian and ethical issues surrounding the trade, cocaine could well rank as the world's most ecologically devastating crop. Its monoculture production on hillsides results first in deforestation then in topsoil erosion: and the pesticides and fertilizers used are washed into ecosystems with adverse effects. And just when it's growing nicely, along come the authorities to slather the growing areas with herbicides. Then there's production: with coca leaves containing only one per cent cocaine, much processing needs to happen to create a marketable substance. This involves sulphuric acid, ether, acetone and kerosene, all of which make it back into the environment too. Combine all of that with the various unpleasant ways in which the final product crosses the Atlantic and cocaine easily merits its position as the least green illegal drug.

Eggs (from chickens)

*L*ook at eggs with the hard, uncompromising stare of either the stern environ-mentalist or vegan and you will conclude that, like all animal protein (see meat, p. 163), they are a highly inefficient way of producing food and we should therefore stop eating them forthwith. It takes about 180 grams of chickenfeed and a great deal of water to create a single 60-gram egg. Far better for the environ-ment if we all ate lentils. The bald fact is that reducing your consumption of animal protein is the single most effective step you can take to reduce the impact of your diet on the environment. But ask for a show of hands willing to renounce eggs completely for the planet and there would be few takers. Britons ate 10 billion eggs in 2004, courtesy of around 30 million laying hens. The culinary and food value of eggs is immense, their contribution to our cuisine incalculable. But given the 3:1 'feed to food' conversion ratio, is there such a thing as a sustainable egg? And behind the environmental cost there's also the inescapable fact that much egg production happens in a way that many find unacceptable: 66 per cent of British eggs are still laid by hens in cages.

Deep green:
Grow your own eggs

In many cases (see chicken, pork, lamb, beef) the keeping of live-stock at home has issues that end up outweighing the environmental benefits. But keeping a few hens for eggs can work well for anyone with a decent-sized garden. Unless you have an even larger area of land on which to grow cereal crops, you will still have to buy in the feed, so home-based hens can rarely be entirely sustainable. But you can minimize the impact of this by making sure the feed is produced organically, which uses less energy, and by supplementing their food with veg scraps. The birds' manure makes excellent fertilizer, so you won't have to buy in as much fertility for the garden in the form of compost or artificial fertilizer; and chickens are good at preparing the ground for growing by scratching away at it and clearing away pests and weed seeds. Each hen will produce around 270 eggs a year, so a small flock will provide you with egg self-sufficiency. For extra eco-points, you can adopt a 'spent' battery hen. Battery layers are slaughtered after around seventy-two weeks, which means millions of hens have to be disposed of each year. 'Adopting' such hens after the farmer has finished with them is a humane and cheap way of getting your own egg supply going.

Dark green:

The cute small farm at the roadside that keeps a few hens and sells surplus eggs

Such places still exist, as attested to by the signs that flash by as you cruise along rural roads. Eggs from these places are unlikely to have organic certification, but it is very possible that the hens that produce them have a nicer life and a lesser environmental impact than eggs certified by one of the less-rigorous organic certification bodies. There's no guarantee, of course: but the proof will be in the quality of the egg. 'Home-grown' eggs have a quality and freshness that even the finest supermarket organic eggs can rarely match.

Quite green:
Organic eggs (Soil Association or Demeter certified)

It is mildly contentious to put organic eggs high up a strictly environmental ranking, especially when intensive chicken production (see p. 60) gets a controversial 'dark green' ranking for its substantially lower energy use. Whilst intensive farming's detractors might point to, say, the high concentrations of acidifying ammonia emitted from a shed packed with 40,000 hens, per-chicken pollutant emissions are similar in organic and conventional systems. The British Egg Information Council contends that it would be possible to reduce ammonia emissions more easily in indoor systems. And despite the vast, complex mechanization of battery sheds, sheer economies of scale mean that organic egg production also uses 14 per cent more energy per tonne of eggs than conventional production. It can also be argued that caged hens experience a mildly improved form of hell compared with intensively reared broilers, who have to shuffle around in their own excrement all day. Some people even make the case that the prison lifestyle at least protects caged hens from death by fox, which contributes to the higher mortality rate amongst organic flocks (10 per cent versus 6 per cent for battery hens). Be all of that as it may, the difference in energy consumption of the organic system is surely outweighed by the advantages of organic chickens: their 85 per cent organic feed provokes the manufacture of few energy-intensive pesticides; they can be integrated into a mixed-farming enterprise; and anyway, the hens have an infinitely better life (and produce a much better product) than their intensive counterparts. The Soil Association and Demeter (biodynamic) organic standards for eggs are currently the most rigorous.

Light green:
Free range

You could argue that the worst free-range systems – with colonies of up to 4,000 birds and perhaps only one 'pop-hole' to the outside world for every 600 – are little better than caged systems in welfare terms. There is little to choose between the two systems in environmental terms either. But that cage issue keeps getting in the way, making it seem right to rank free range higher. (The Soil Association standard, by the way, allows a maximum colony size of 500 but frequently grants exceptions up to 2,000 birds.)

Pale green:
Barn

This accounts for only 7 per cent of British egg production and whilst hens are at least freed from their cages, they can be packed very tightly at densities of 9–25 hens per square metre. It is also harder to manage wastes and diseases in barn systems, which arguably makes them only marginally greener than 'laying cages'.

Not even a little bit green:
Battery ('laying cage') eggs

This system is relatively energy-efficient and the hens' environment, behaviour and potential diseases can be easily controlled. Inputs of food and water and outputs of eggs and manure are all managed automatically, with great efficiency. So from one perspective this is an environmentally friendly method of food production. But hens, descended from wild jungle fowl, were not put on this earth to be caged for a year then slaughtered, even if their new 'enriched' cages offer 750 square centimetres per bird and a perching and scratching area. It may objectively be 14 per cent more energy-efficient than organic production, but this small advantage is surely eroded by the mechanized and intensive nature of battery farming, which requires complex infrastructure and creates localized pollution; and by the sheer inhumanity of caging birds on such a massive scale to create food.

MORE INFORMATION:
Give a home to a battery hen: www.thehenshouse.co.uk
Reports about the egg industry available from Compassion in World Farming: www.ciwf.org.uk **and Sustain:** www.sustainweb.org
Information from the British egg industry: www.britegg.co.uk

Electricity

*E*co-fundamentalists might venture that electricity can never be 'green'. They *have a point: it's mostly generated by fossil fuels in the UK, in huge, central-ized power stations which lose over 60 per cent of the 'primary' energy they produce, mostly as heat vented up through cooling towers and also in transmis-sion and distribution. Most of us would agree, however, that electricity is far too useful to do without. Green options are tricky, though: whilst solar panels and wind turbines can be pretty and offer a relatively eco-friendly way of generating electricity, they remain expensive and often impractical for domestic use. The boring truth is that reducing your electricity use is the easiest and best way to make a positive impact: it's not worth even thinking about 'microgeneration' until you have taken every possible step to do this. Solar PVs and plasma TVs would be uneasy bedfellows indeed.*

Deep green:
Totally Amish

The absence of electricity is not entirely incompatible with twenty-first-century life, as certain American religious communities prove. Go without electricity and you knock out up to 25 per cent of your total household energy consumption and up to half your CO_2 emis-sions from energy use, as well as sparing Gaia the impact of manufacturing and disposing of all those electrical appliances. There are electricity-free substitutes for most of our conveniences (fridges, washing machines, central heating); however, they usually involve either a drastic drop in quality, a massive hike in effort, their own adverse ecological effects or all three. And whilst life with no electronic media beyond a wind-up radio may be paradise for some, others may crave a sneaky bicycle-powered charger to juice up the laptop and mobile phone.

Dark green:
Grid-connected microgeneration plus green-tariff electricity

A combination of good green-tariff electricity (see below) and micro-generation presents you with a very real prospect of being not only carbon-neutral but 'carbon-negative' – a net contributor to the total stock of UK renewable energy. And unlike 'off-grid' microgeneration, this option means you can fall back into the big strong arms of the electricity grid, using it like a giant battery. However, in the event of a power cut your solar panels or wind turbine won't turn the lights back on (which is kind of disappointing, given the feeling of energy-independence that such devices inspire). It is possible to generate as much as you consume, although it takes five-figure sums to reach the wattage needed. So grid-connected microgeneration is something that is currently done out of a sense of environmental altruism. No one is in it for the money: solar photovoltaic cells are still expensive and small wind turbines perform very poorly in the urban areas in which most of us live. Even with grants from the Department for Business, Enterprise and Regulatory Reform's Low Carbon Buildings Programme, rising fuel prices and the fact that you can sell electricity and Renewables Obligation Certificates, payback times still stretch into many decades.

Quite green:
Green-tariff electricity

Microgeneration is out of reach for many of us, either because of the cost or the fact that we lack south-facing roofs, windy spots with planning permission or reliable private rivers. If you still hanker after renewable energy, though, green-tariff electricity is by far the easiest option and arguably the greenest. However, there is a huge difference between the greenness of different suppliers, tariffs change frequently and (at the time of writing) there is no reliable guide since Friends of the Earth stopped publishing one in 2003. The key issue is that the Renewables Obligation forces all suppliers to source a gradually increasing percentage of their electricity from renewable sources, so buying 'green' may just be helping them to meet their obligations and not in fact increasing the demand for renewables. Good Energy, Green Energy and Ecotricity have no fossil-fuel or nuclear baggage and have been rated highly for greenness in the past.

Light green:
Off-grid

It's perfectly legal to unhook your electricity supply and generate your own, should you wish. However, unless you live near a suitable spot for a bit of micro-hydroelectricity, the first thing to bear in mind is that renewable energy sources like wind and solar photovoltaic will not provide a constant supply. Which means back-up, in the form of hefty lead-acid batteries or a generator, should you wish to watch TV of a calm winter's evening. The environmental impact of all this kit, plus the fact that you won't be donating your surplus to others via the National Grid, is what demotes this 'run for the hills' approach to electricity to mere 'light green' status. And whilst it is theoretically possible to generate as much electricity as you are likely to use over a year with wind and solar (the UK family average is 3,300kWh), getting the oomph needed to run hungry appliances like washing machines means heavy-duty electrical systems. So it's most practical to combine off-gridness with serious energy-saving lifestyle changes, which puts it high on the 'hair shirt' scale.

Pale green:
Domestic CHP

Combined heat and power (CHP) systems use the waste heat from heating systems to generate electricity. On a domestic scale, this means a fancy gas boiler incorporating a Sterling Engine, in which pistons powered by the heating and cooling of gas move through an alternator. Why does this high-tech, fossil-fuel-based idea get green points? Because it gets round the major problem of energy loss in electricity generation (see introduction). CHP can operate at up to 90 per cent efficiency and manufacturers claim 25 per cent savings on energy bills and a 20 per cent reduction in household CO_2 emissions. It's a new market, though, with few products currently available (see below for suppliers). For carbon-neutral CHP, there are systems that run off biofuels – but you wouldn't want one in the house.

Not even a little bit green:
Business as usual, plus turning everything on at peak times

Electricity generation is not only a woeful 40 per cent efficient because of the heat loss and transfer issues; it is also, in the UK at least, largely powered by fossil fuels (40 per cent gas, 33 per cent coal) and nuclear fission (19 per cent). Both of these have environmental implications that unsettle most people – and the biosphere – to differing degrees. Less than 4 per cent of our electricity currently comes from renewable sources. So doing nothing is definitely at the bottom of the green scale, although climate-change sceptics and people hell-bent on increasing their carbon footprint might like to take things a step further by switching their heating over to electric bar fires (see p. 141). And to really trash things, switch 'em on at peak times (say just after *Coronation Street*, when the nation is making a cup of tea), thus boosting peak demand and the probability that the National Grid will have to crank up one of its standby coal-fired power stations to stop the lights going out.

MORE INFORMATION
Comparison of green-tariff electricity providers from Ethical Consumer: www.ethiscore.org
Information on microgeneration: www.cat.org.uk
Government schemes supporting microgeneration: www.lowcarbonbuildings.org.uk
Domestic CHP: www.microgen.com, www.whispergen.com

Fish and shellfish

Walk into the fishmonger's shop and you enter an ethical and environmental minefield. Fish is, of course, terribly good for us, with oily species such as mackerel and salmon (see p. 220) providing the best source of the omega-3 fatty acids that are so important to human health. However, there is a big question mark over how long this source of superb healthy food will be around. The global fish catch increased five-fold in the second half of the twentieth century. Today, only a quarter of fish are not in trouble: 52 per cent of the world's stocks are being fished to the limits of their biological productivity, 16 per cent are overexploited and 8 per cent are depleted or recovering from depletion. Fishing does more than just deplete wild fish populations, though: it destroys the marine environment and kills untargeted species through by-catch too. Fish farming – aquaculture – is not necessarily the answer to this marine pillage, mainly because of the feed-conversion problem. Many of the farmed fish we eat in Britain are carnivorous and at least 2 kilos of feed based on wild fish is needed to produce a single kilo of farmed fish. And that's only one of the problems with aquaculture. So how is the conscientious greenie to navigate this fishy minefield? There are guides available (see below) and this entry acts as a primer to the subject.

Deep green:
No fish

It may not be the most gastronomically acceptable or even the ealthiest option, but giving up (or not starting to eat) fish is arguably the most eco-friendly. You will be relieving pressure on beleaguered fish stocks and marine ecosystems and not contributing to aquaculture, which can be destructive. Whilst they are enormously beneficial to health, fish oils are not essential and can be replaced with the omega-3 oils from flax (linseed) oil, rapeseed oil, walnuts, the meat and milk of pasture-fed cows and pasture-fed lamb and venison.

Dark green:
Wild fish, sustainably caught

Harvesting a sustainable amount of food from the wild is always the greenest way to eat, because nature does the otherwise ecologically expensive job of creating food for the thing you are harvesting. Feeding your food is a major contributor to farming's environmental impact, whether it's manufacturing fertilizer for plants or growing feed for farmed creatures. Many wild fish, of course, are not sustainably caught and the failure to recover of the once-abundant Grand Banks cod fishery off Newfoundland shows how serious an issue this is. But in recognition of the parlous state of the world's fish stocks, there are a growing number of fisheries being certified as sustainable by the Marine Stewardship Council. Although not entirely without its problems, this scheme gives the best guarantee that your fish has been wrested from the ocean in a way that doesn't damage the overall stock or the environment. See below for lists of which fish are 'safe' to buy and which fisheries have been certified by the MSC.

Quite green:
Herbivorous farmed fish, or shellfish from sustainable aquaculture

There is such a thing as sustainable aquaculture, but it does limit your choice somewhat. Herbivorous fish do not have as severe a feed-conversion problem as carnivores like salmon, sea bass or trout; however neither, sadly, do they have the gastronomic glamour. Tilapia can be farmed in reasonably sustainable systems (in warmer countries) but large concentrations of fish in small areas cannot help but have some environmental impact. Carp are a better bet, in that they have some omega-3 content and can be farmed locally. Carp farming has yet to catch on in Britain, but is common in continental Europe and has sustained many in Asia, where it has been integrated into livestock and arable farming for millennia. Shellfish are less problematic when farmed: as filter feeders they demand pure water and unless they are grown very intensively they have a relatively low environmental impact. Mussels, oysters and clams are the main farmed species.

Not even a little bit green:
Unsustainably caught wild fish

In the introduction to his book *The End of the Line*, author Charles Clover uses a vivid analogy to illustrate the effect of trawling. He envisages two immense all-terrain vehicles dragging a vast weighted net across the African savannah: the net crushes all before it, leaving behind a wasteland; and it catches all living things in its path, many of which are then discarded, unwanted. Unsustainable fishing is not just about exploiting a natural resource faster than it can regenerate. It's also about the destruction of the seabed and its fragile, important ecosystems by trawling; and the depletion of other species such as albatross and dolphins that end up as by-catch. Sadly, many of the species we know and love to eat are now classified as endangered: North Atlantic cod (see p. 72), skate, monkfish, plaice, bluefin tuna. Unless it's indicated otherwise, it is safe to assume that any wild fish you are buying has been fished unsustainably. However, for some of these species there are sustainable fisheries: see the link below.

Not even a little bit green 2:
Fish from unsustainable aquaculture

At its worst, fish farming has impacts that make even the direst live-stock farms seem like a good idea environmentally. The tight concentrations of penned fish create concentrations of effluent and, in the case of salmon, make the creatures prone to parasitic infesta-tions which are often treated with pesticides. Wild fish are affected by the parasites and can also be genetically weakened by inter-breeding with escaped farmed fish. And then there's the feed-conversion problem: with salmon it's 3 kilos of feed to one kilo of farmed fish; with other fish it can be even higher. There are certi-fied organic fish farms that use much lower stocking densities, no hazardous chemicals and seek to minimize ecological damage: but they still can't get round the unsustainable feed-conversion problem.

MORE INFORMATION
Marine Conservation Society website with information on sustainable fish: www.fishonline.org

Flowers

*I*sn't there anything nice that doesn't come loaded with ecological issues? No, not really. Flowers, the universal symbols of love, peace, benevolence and good vibes, have even more environmental baggage than most lovely things. The reasons are straightforward. We like to have a big selection of delightful flowers at all times, especially in late winter (Valentine's Day). Our climate doesn't allow for British favourites like the rose, carnation, chrysanthemum and freesia to be grown all year round, but modern technology can get round the problem easily. So flowers are often grown in heated greenhouses or imported from hotter countries. Today, Britain imports 85 per cent of its flowers in a business that is worth more than the music industry. This unleashes all manner of eco-nasties: CO_2 emissions from heating greenhouses, air-freighting and refrigeration; heavy pesticide use; excessive water abstraction; and impacts on important ecosystems.

Deep green:
Grow your own

Nurturing the perfect rose is not for everyone. But if flowers are your thing – and especially if you have a greenhouse of some description – then there can be floral loveliness, of one sort or another, nearly all year round. It goes without saying that deep green growers will be staying away from artificial chemicals and heating; and thus they are likely to be making a net environmental contribution, in particular by providing forage for insects. Add a beehive or two into the mix and the flowers make an edible as well as an aesthetic contribution to the household.

Dark green:
The occasional wild forage

Obviously, the heavy depletion of wild or even parkland flowers is not particularly eco-friendly, neighbourly or in some cases even legal. But in mid to late spring, summer and autumn there are plenty of things that can be picked with a clear conscience and look great in a vase, from volunteer oilseed rape to elderflower, flowering weeds and wild berries. A wild bunch may not last long: but it costs nothing in either financial or environmental terms if carefully chosen.

Quite green:
Buy local, seasonal, naturally grown flowers and pot plants

This is harder than it sounds, as there is no requirement to label flowers' country of origin. In practice it will mean quizzing the florist or local nursery and buying cut flowers in a season that starts with spring daffodils (of which Britain is an exporter) and ends in the late summer.

Light green:
Buy 'certified' imported flowers

In the face of awakening consumer concern about the impacts of the flower industry (see below), various certification systems for flowers have been introduced. You can now buy Fairtrade flowers: these guarantee that certain levels of workers' rights and environmental performance have been met; and they ensure that 8 per cent of the export value goes back into community projects. Whether or not

Fairtrade, when applied to flowers, guarantees a truly sustainable industry is a moot point; but its produce is surely better than flowers that lack the certification. Flowers with the EU-backed Fair Flowers Fair Plants certification, which offers similar environmental and working-practice guarantees, are now becoming available in the UK.

Not particularly green:
Imported, out-of-season flowers from hot climates, lacking any certification

A study commissioned by Sainsbury's and supplier World Flowers and carried out by Cranfield University showed, perhaps surprisingly, that a sample batch of air-freighted Kenyan flowers produced one-fifth of the CO_2 of an equivalent consignment of Dutch hothouse flowers, even allowing for the dreaded 'radiative forcing' multiplier (see p. 5). So does this mean, as the UK government suggested on the back of this study, that buying African flowers will reduce your environmental impact? Floriculture is Kenya's second most important export industry and directly employs up to 70,000 people. Intensive growing, however, results in poor conditions for workers and severe environmental problems, the best known of which are the dire impacts on Lake Naivasha, around which much Kenyan flower-growing is based. As with other plants, it makes CO_2 sense to take advantage of a hot climate. But does it makes overall ecological and economic sense to import such an environmentally demanding luxury crop from a fragile and water-stressed region? It is a very thorny issue.

Not particularly green 2:

Hothouse flowers

With a journey of no more than a few hundred miles rather than several thousand, flower miles are much less of an issue for plants grown in greenhouses. But the Cranfield study estimated that the gas and electricity needed to grow 12,000 cut rose stems in a heated greenhouse resulted in the emission of 35 tonnes of CO_2, five times the Kenyan batch. And with lower yields than in Africa, the overall difference in environmental impact is magnified further. So if the Cranfield study is representative – and if CO_2 is the main concern – then European hothouse flowers come at the bottom of the green scale. But with the concept of green taking in other environmental impacts, such as effects on local ecosystems, there's probably little to choose between the two.

Fridges and freezers

*W*here are fridges and freezers in the green scheme of things? They have a bad rep from the pre-1994 days when their refrigerant was made of ozone-depleting CFCs; and more recently from the 'fridge mountains' created when new regulations on eco-friendly disposal were first introduced. Fridges and freezers suck up power – 3 per cent of household energy and up to 18 per cent of domestic electricity, not to mention all the embodied energy expended in building them. And without them, the crazy modern food chain – with its fridge-friendly convenience foods sold in impersonal, out-of-town mega-sheds – would not exist. Maybe we'd be living in a 'slow-food' paradise, all happily haggling down the market every day for fresh produce grown on lovely local farms. Or perhaps we'd all be dying of scurvy. Bash them all you like, fridges and freezers have given us a more varied, reliable and predictable range of nutrients throughout the year. The ozone hole is sorted, pretty much; and the WEEE directive means that manufacturers and importers will be responsible for recycling as of mid-2007. And life without a decent frozen margarita would be grim indeed.

Deep green:
No fridge

To the hardest of hardcore greenies, refrigeration is an unnecessary high-tech evil that puts us at one remove from real fresh food. Produce is at its peak when it's completely fresh from the plant or the creature; fridges simply preside over a gradual decline in nutritional value whilst contributing to global warming. The no-fridge lifestyle is easy for the committed urbanite, who has constant access to bijou shops and markets, but harder for rural refrigerophobes, who will need advanced smallholding skills (or spend most of their life travelling to and from supermarkets) in order to keep up a supply of reasonably fresh produce.

Dark green:
Zeer pot

For those who want the luxury of home food cooling but are off-grid or otherwise worried about the 170–600+ kWh per year a fridge will consume, there's the low-tech 'pot-in-pot' approach. Based on ancient technology and refined more recently to help the rural poor in Nigeria, the 'zeer pot' consists of a terracotta pot within another, larger pot. A layer of sand in between the two is kept moist, the contents are covered with a cloth and the evaporation of the water cools the inner pot and its contents. Simple, effective and without the hassle of extended warranties and annoying gurgling noises, it will save you money and at least 80kg of CO_2 emissions each year.

Quite green:
Pantry and root cellar, A++-rated larder fridge, A+-rated chest freezer

This is a rather eclectic mix of technologies, but it's the best combination for your food and not too bad for the environment. A pantry and root cellar will take care of all those things that would really rather not be in the desiccated fridge environment but so often are: root veg, green veg and salads, potatoes, fruit, cheese, butter. This will free up the small, ultra-efficient larder fridge (examples of which use as little as 84kWh per year) for the things a fridge is really for: white wine and beer and maybe fresh meat and fish. (Of course if you're teetotal, hardcore, vegan or all three, you could just do without the fridge or use a zeer pot.) An efficient chest freezer can then be used solely for its strengths: extending the season of your own fruit and vegetable crops and dealing with any surpluses; and keeping that half-a-pig you ordered from the smallholder up the road. The combined power consumption of these two appliances is a little more than the fridge/freezer below, but the impact of the big freezer on your shopping habits could well cancel this out.

Light green:
A + +-rated fridge/freezer with low annual energy usage, HFC-free

All fridges and freezers must by law carry an energy-efficiency rating, which now stretches from A++ (best) to G (worst). It's a little bit misleading, though: fridge/freezers can be energy-efficient and still guzzle loads of power if they also happen to be huge. Mighty American-style 'side-by-side' fridge/freezers, the SUVs of the domestic refrigeration world, can carry an A rating but can also guzzle over 600kWh per year, twice the consumption of similarly rated but more humble appliances. So looking for the lowest annual energy usage (which must also be printed on the energy label) as well as the best efficiency will get you the most environmentally friendly fridge. Choose HFC-free fridges and freezers too: whilst HFCs may not nuke the ozone layer like their predecessors CFCs, they are stupendously potent global-warming gases and fridges using hydro-carbon-based refrigerants such as R600a are much less of a disaster area. See below for how to track down the greenest fridges and freezers.

Not even a little bit green:

Old fridge/freezer, kept nice and dirty and next to a radiator, then smashed up and thrown on a skip when it finally breaks down

If it's old, then your fridge/freezer is probably less energy-efficient than modern models in the first place. Its insulation is probably failing, which will make things worse; and to really crank up its consumption you could put it next to a radiator so it has to fight extra hard to stay cool. Keeping the coils at the back nice and dusty will make it even less efficient by further preventing its refrigerant from dissipating heat. However, really to trash the planet with your old fridge, set about it with a sledgehammer when it's replacement time, releasing the ecocidal refrigerants within to wreak their havoc on the atmosphere. Please note this is now illegal as well as daft.

MORE INFORMATION
Ethical Consumer: www.ethicalconsumer.org

Fruit and veg

(see also: bananas, p.20; oranges, p. 186; apples, p. 9; strawberries, p. 233; potatoes, p. 209; salads, p. 216; courgettes, p. 90; peas, p. 193; tomatoes, p. 255)

It's easy to think of fruit and veg as generally environmentally benign, what with their 'five a day' status as the holy grail of healthy eating. They certainly place less stress on the biosphere than animals farmed for meat, whose voracious appetites mean that most of the world's arable agriculture is currently geared up to growing food for livestock rather than people. The end result of this feed-conversion issue is that a given amount of meat can contain a great many 'embodied' resources, such as irrigation water, fertilizers and pesticides. Fruit and veg are pretty hungry and thirsty, too, though: even in the most ecologically groovy ultra-organic systems they need imported fertility, which means vast quantities of animal manures or compost. As with so many environmental issues, it's about inputs and outputs: you can't coax a plant into producing energy- and mineral-rich leaves, fruit or seed without giving it plenty of 'food'. So 'green' fruit and veg needs to be sustainably fed; and then there are the many more highly publicized issues such as seasonality, agrochemicals, food miles and 'protected' cropping.

Deep green:

Grow your own

What if we did grow all our own fruit and veg? It could, arguably, be a bit of an ecological disaster. There are many efficiencies and economies of scale to be had in larger-scale horticulture, from high-tech but frugal drip irrigation systems to the simple fact that experienced, professional growers get much better yields. And quite how a doorstep manure-delivery system that is both efficient and acceptable in environmental terms could work remains to be seen. And yet – as long as we don't all try to be self-sufficient – growing a few things that can otherwise have a great big eco-bootprint is no bad idea. Salads, tomatoes and apples are just a few examples of easy-to-grow produce that can otherwise involve, variously, a great deal of refrigeration, food miles, irrigation and agrochemicals.

Dark green:
Seasonal, local, probably organic

And probably in that order, too. If fruit or veg is in season, then its growth will not have demanded artificial energy: the sun will have done the job. If it's local, then its transport will have used less energy and a side benefit of that is that its nutrient content may well be higher. If it's organic, then in most cases less energy will have been used to grow the crop because no (or minimal) industrially produced fertilizers or agrochemicals will have been used. And there will have been correspondingly fewer releases into the environment – and residues in the final product – of toxic substances. (However, in environmental and health terms, the importance of the organic issue varies for different items of produce – check the individual entries for the detail.)

Quite green:
Sea-freighted seasonal imports, preferably organic and/or Fairtrade

Not all food miles are equal; and arguably, not all are bad. There is a certain logic in taking advantage of someone else's warmer climate in our own cold season; and obviously with crops such as oranges and bananas we take advantage of hotter climates to eat things that would otherwise be unobtainable. It's mainly to do with the mode of transport: in energy terms, shipping is 100 times more efficient per tonne/kilometre than air freight. So those New Zealand apples, which come by sea to plug our own seasonal gap, are perhaps not as bad as you might think and may compare favourably with a more local apple that has been kept in refrigerated storage for many months. Organic produce will have been grown with fewer energy-intensive inputs and Fairtrade certification tends to mean that the farm will be a smaller-scale operation. Examples of sea-freighted seasonal imports include citrus fruits, bananas, apples, kiwi fruit: in general, heavy produce that can be refrigerated.

Pale green:
Out-of-season local produce

There are traditional ways of cheating the seasons: pickling, preserving and drying were all used by our forebears to make sure that warm-season produce remained available in some form or other through the cooler months. However, if you want fresh produce out of season, some sort of technology is needed, from a simple polytunnel to a high-tech heated greenhouse. Indoor growing has some environmental advantages: for example easier disease control means fewer pesticides; irrigation water can be recycled; and growers can even take advantage of the waste heat from factories by siting glasshouses next to them. However, in the depths of winter, local crops grown with artificial heat have a heavy energy demand that puts them on a similar eco-footing to those that have rumbled up the motorways from southern Europe. Some examples of out-of-season local produce: tomatoes, strawberries, cucumbers, celery.

Not particularly green:
Out-of-season road-freighted imports

If it's from somewhere else in Europe, say a heated Dutch glasshouse or an unheated Spanish polytunnel, then chances are it has come by road. Trucking is a great deal better than air freight in energy terms, but it still uses ten times more energy for a given weight of fruit and veg than shipping. Some out-of-season trucked imports: broccoli, tomatoes, courgettes.

Not even a little bit green:
Air-freighted imports

Even if it's been grown by eco-monks whose environmental footprint is smaller than that of a Bhutanese subsistence farmer, if it's fresh food that has come in by air, it ain't green. Air-freighted fresh produce is the least necessary and most polluting per tonne-kilometre. If the survival of humanity depended on our eating mangetout in December, then maybe we could find a way to justify it. But it doesn't, so it's hard to. Air-freighted food tends to be well out of season, light and quickly perishable, for example French beans, blueberries, asparagus.

MORE INFORMATION
List of farmers' markets: www.farmersmarkets.net

Furniture

*A*re *you sitting greenly? Unless you have a serious, compulsive furniture-buying habit or always insist on the least green products (see below), furniture accounts for a small chunk of household environmental impact. It doesn't necessarily have a great deal of embodied energy or toxicity (i.e. the impacts that result from its production); and unless it is made of the very worst materials, doesn't create any extra pollution during its lifetime. There is still, however, a big gulf between the eco-footprint of the deep greenie's hard hessian sofa and the plush luxury enjoyed by those with more plutocratic tendencies.*

Deep green:
Salvage and DIY

This gives you an opportunity to ascend to the giddy heights of greenness by becoming a 'waste importer'. Whether it's beaten-up pallets, discarded car seats or unwanted floorboards, the tips and skips of Britain abound with material that could be knocked up into decent furniture with a modicum of skill and effort (and then probably sold at a vast profit in a trendy London shop).

Dark green:
Second-hand furniture

Even if your new chairs are made from the most politically correct wood imaginable and crafted by the most conscientious, right-on eco-elves using traditional, low-impact techniques, they will still make a small dent in the biosphere. One could argue, for example, that the poor tree that was sacrificed could have been left to see out its days naturally and then provide valuable insect habitat after its death. Or that the elves' chisels have some embodied energy. But this irreverent nitpicking illustrates that there is little to choose between the very best new furniture and second-hand. The benefit of buying second-hand, as with many things, is that you are diluting even further any energy that was used to create the furniture in the first place, and saving the chairs from landfill or incineration.

Quite green:
New furniture made from natural, sustainable materials

That groovy 1960s plastic seating pod that hangs from the ceiling may have a certain designer cachet, but it would take a long time to degrade in landfill and would kick out a nasty cocktail of pollutants if incinerated. Furniture with Forest Stewardship Council (FSC) certification currently gives the best guarantee that its wood comes from a sustainable forest. Natural materials such as wool and linen are, essentially, low-impact agricultural crops, although some natural fabrics, particularly cotton (see p. 70), have their issues. Choosing organic materials for large items like mattresses will mean there is minimal risk of exposure to pesticide residues. Such furniture is likely to have a long life and can be more easily recycled or disposed of in a way which minimizes environmental impact.

Pale green:
New furniture from companies with strong, credible environmental policies

Whether deep greenies like it or not, artificial materials are pivotal to the modern world. Imagine life without Velcro. Whilst there are natural, or almost natural, alternatives to almost any artificial furnishing material – lino instead of vinyl flooring, for example – there will often need to be manufactured or petroleum-based inputs to furniture. The classic case study for an industrial company that has carried on being industrial but has balanced its activities with a raft of sustainability measures is US carpet company Interface, Inc., whose chairman Ray Anderson had an abrupt, Damascene eco-conversion some years ago. Closer to home, Swedish retailer IKEA, loved and loathed by Britons in equal measure, is well rated for its clear policy of making sure the wood it uses is not from old-growth forests or those with high conservation value.

Not terribly green:
Vast expanses of leather

Leather is a renewable and biodegradable resource, of course; but cattle are much more expensive to raise, in environmental terms, than trees (see also meat, p. 163). And getting leather into a state in which it will provide maximum sofa comfort involves tanning and preparation processes which use many resources and generate much waste.

Not even a little bit green:
Furniture made from untraceable tropical hardwoods

The story of tropical forests is well documented and rather depressing. The lungs of the planet and havens of immense biodiversity, they are under constant threat from clear-cutting in order to plant cash crops such as palm oil and soya; and from illegal logging. The present rate of deforestation, which has seen half the world's forest cover already removed, outstrips the ability of forests to regenerate. The best way to avoid contributing to this sad state of affairs is scrupulously to avoid tropical hardwoods such as teak and mahogany, because unless the vendor has a paper trail that can trace your chair right back to a tree that was felled legitimately, there is a strong chance that the wood was cut illegally and unsustainably.

Not even a little bit green either:
Furniture packed with (or made from) iffy chemicals

Whether or not brominated flame retardants have health issues is currently subject to the usual game of tennis between the chemical industry (who say there are no health issues) and concerned pressure groups (who say there are plenty of health issues). Whilst the EU continues to be happy with the widely used retardant Deca-BDE, Sweden has banned it and at least one American state has concerns over it, because of its persistence in the environment. Deca-BDE has been found in polar bears, not known for their need of sofas. The wholesomeness or otherwise of vinyl or PVC is also the subject of debate; but there is no question that its manufacture involves some extremely unpleasant substances nor that it can 'off-gas' equally unpleasant substances through its lifespan.

Greenhouses

*W*ill the embodied energy of the materials that make up your greenhouse be offset by the food miles you will save by growing your own produce in it? Or will your inefficient gardening techniques cancel this out? Sometimes it is possible to get a little bit too bogged down in shades-of-greenery detail. Like anything man-made, greenhouses do have an energy cost. But this does vary according to your preferred choice of venue for protected horticulture.

Deep green:
Wood-framed lean-to conservatory, built against the house

The most eco-friendly thing you can do with a greenhouse is not to let all the valuable warm air it generates go to waste at the bottom of the garden. So if possible, building a lean-to conservatory against the (preferably south-facing) wall of your house has all sorts of environmental advantages. The stone walls will keep the conservatory warmer at night and through the year, extending the range and season of things you can grow. And it will act as a thermal 'buffer space', whose sun-warmed air can help to keep the house warmer in the cooler months and thus lower your heating bills. Wood (see below) has much lower embodied energy than either metal or plastic and therefore makes a greener choice of material for the frame.

Dark green:
Wooden greenhouse

These are more expensive than aluminium, which is most commonly used for greenhouse frames. But they do have some advantages. Wooden greenhouses are warmer, overall, holding out the prospect of better yields and reducing your fuel costs should you have been so un-green as to heat the greenhouse. And, of course, wood is a renewable material, with the energy used in its production in the hundreds of kilowatt-hours per tonne, compared with 27,000kWh per tonne for energy-intensive aluminium. The choice of wood is important, too. Clearly local wood is better, but softwoods of the sort that grow quickly and cheaply in Europe need to be treated. This no longer involves carcinogenic creosote or troubling arsenic, both of which are restricted by EU legislation; however, it does involves pressure treatment with pesticides that are toxic to fish and wildlife. An alternative is to go for Western Red Cedar, which has natural resistance to decay but may have travelled here all the way from Canada.

Quite green:
Aluminium greenhouse

It may be made of aluminium, but so are most bicycles (see p. 42) and they're still pretty green.

Light green:
Polytunnel

They may excite nimbyist ire in areas where they pop up on a large, industrial scale to feed our insatiable national strawberry habit, but polytunnels are often at the centre of the very greenest smallholdings. The main reason is cost: a monster 90-foot-long polytunnel can be yours for the price of a tiny posh greenhouse. So for those looking for the 'Good Life', polytunnels make financial sense. They end up at the bottom of the greenhouse scale for two reasons: materials and lifespan. Polytunnels use aluminium frames and plastic covers, both of which contain vast amounts of embodied energy, and whilst they can both be recycled, this too is an energy-intensive process. The plastic sheeting has a relatively short life because it is degraded by ultraviolet radiation, meaning that tunnels need to be re-skinned after as little as four years. However, assuming you use low-impact growing techniques, these energy costs will be more than cancelled out by the reduced food miles and general green value of growing your own.

Heating
(space and water)

After transport, British homes are the next biggest users of our national energy supply, accounting for 30 per cent of it; and heating and hot water account for the bulk (82 per cent) of this. So apart from leaving the Learjet in the hangar, saving energy on home heating is just about the greenest thing we average punters can do, particularly in terms of reducing CO_2 emissions. Interestingly, although the use of central heating has rocketed since the 1970s and our homes are on average 6°C warmer inside now than they were then, the total energy we use to heat our homes has not risen very much, thanks to increases in energy efficiency and insulation. There remain, however, huge savings to be made. Most of our houses are, to a greater or lesser degree, ecological disaster zones because they are poorly insulated, badly orientated in relation to the sun, or have old-fashioned heating equipment. A house can in theory stay cosy with just a quarter of the energy currently needed by the average dwelling; and a super-insulated eco-house can get by with even less. The problem is that 'retrofitting' energy efficiency to your house can be a hugely expensive business. So, as with many things, the very greenest options involve either maximum privation or maximum expense. But there are shades in between that may suit us all.

Deep green 1:
Shiver and smell

You save 10 per cent on your heating bill for every degree the thermostat goes down: why not knock it all the way from a typical 21°C to a borderline-bearable 16°C (the legal minimum for seated workers) and save 50 per cent? With other hardcore austerity measures, like weekly showering and never heating bedrooms, you can dramatically reduce your carbon footprint and energy bills for zero outlay. Brrr. Just like the 1950s.

Deep green 2:
'Retrofit' to the max

Greening up an existing house beats a new-build eco-house because it takes up no new land and involves much less energy and fewer materials. Reaching the 75 per cent reduction in energy use that is possible can be expensive, though, and depends on your house. Pre-1930s houses tend to be single-glazed and to lack cavity walls that can be filled with insulation, so it will be expensive to sort out the walls and windows, through which around 50 per cent of heat loss happens. And if you get little sun, then there won't be much help from passive solar heating (see below). Still, with thick insulation all round, high-tech glazing, maybe a pellet-fed biofuel boiler and mechanical heat-recovery systems, 24 Acacia Avenue could become a carbon-neutral eco-home, albeit at a price. There are of course many degrees of retrofitting to suit all houses and budgets, from simple draughtstripping to complicated insulated cladding. See 'More Information' for details.

Dark green:

A new-build eco-house, featuring superinsulation, passive solar, a single, biofuel heat source and solar hot water

This may be the thermal holy grail to which many greenies aspire, but it gets knocked off the top spot for sheer impracticability. It's hardly green to build new houses everywhere, or to demolish your old one; nor is doing so an option available to most of us. However, if you can do it, the lifetime energy savings will easily cancel out at least the carbon impact of a new-build eco-house. Build a house from scratch with minimal energy use in mind and you can swaddle it in ultra-thick insulation, orientate it so the sun does most of the heating work (passive solar), and use high-tech systems to keep it airtight yet comfortable. In the smaller rooms of such a house, the 80W kicked out by a sofa-bound human can be enough to keep it warm; overall, the most you are likely to need is a wood-burning stove – a carbon-neutral heat source – for the darkest, chilliest days. Bear in mind that if you want to go a stage further and grow your own sustainable fuel, even supplying an eco-house like this would need up to a hectare of woodland and advanced coppicing skills. Solar thermal panels will keep the water warm for much of the year, though.

Quite green:

Ground-source heat pump and maximum energy efficiency

Ground-source heat uses refrigeration technology working backwards to concentrate the constant 10°C or so of underground heat to house-warming temperature. Whilst this is potentially very eco-friendly over its lifetime, it's expensive to install, requires a big garden or deep boreholes for the pipes that transfer the underground heat, only works with low-temperature radiators or underfloor heating, and needs a house with superb thermal performance to be worthwhile. And it needs electricity to power the complex gubbins that makes it work, so unless you can power this with renewables, state-of-the-art gas technology may be just as green. Ground-source heat can make economic sense for those without mains gas, though.

Light green:
Gas CHP, maximum energy efficiency

Combined heat and power (CHP) technology for domestic use is only just emerging from fairyland, but it offers highly efficient space- and water-heating plus on-site electricity generation to boot (see electricity, p. 109). It goes without saying that to make this worthwhile, your house should be insulated to within an inch of its life and your family practising all energy-efficient behaviours known to man.

Pale green:
Gas condensing boiler, maximum energy efficiency

This is the best 'real-world' heating option for those of us with access to gas. Condensing boilers operate at up to 90 per cent efficiency, 10 per cent better than the best conventional boilers. And if your boiler is over 10 years old, replacing it with a condensing boiler could pay back in as little as three years, assuming gas prices remain constant, which they won't. Combine this with as many energy-efficiency measures as you can bear, and you'll make a decent-sized dent in your carbon footprint.

Not green:
Coal

Warm, cosy, evocative, snug; also ludicrously inefficient (up to 85 per cent of the heat from a coal fire goes up the chimney), nearly twice as carbon-intensive as gas and with an additional payload of nasty pollutants. As anything other than an occasional winter indulgence, coal can never be green.

Not even a little bit green:
No insulation, electric bar fires

There's a display in London's Science Museum in which you try to work a one-bar electric fire with an exercise bike: the effort it takes to create even a paltry amount of heat is humbling. With electricity generation only 40 per cent efficient, (see electricity, p. 109), even state-of-the-art forms of electric space- and water-heating are worse than gas. Something really inefficient like a three-bar electric fire uses 3kW at full power, which is like having three kettles boiling constantly. Let all this heat escape through an uninsulated house and you have a recipe for both penury and ecological disaster.

MORE INFORMATION
Information on energy saving available from the Centre for Alternative Technology: www.cat.org.uk
Rankings of boiler efficiency available from the Energy Saving Trust: www.est.org.uk
Two 'eco retrofit' houses: Nottingham Ecohome, www.msarch.co.uk/ecohome;

The Yellow House, www.theyellowhouse.org.uk
An 'eco new-build': Tree House, www.treehouseclapham.org

Holidays

Holidays are where the wagging finger of the finger-wagging environmentalist wags most vigorously. Why? Because to the grimmest greenies, the holidays we take today are an unnecessary luxury that damages the environment in almost every way conceivable. Thanks mainly to the carbon-intensity of air travel, they account for around 10 per cent of a Briton's annual carbon footprint. And at the holiday destination, the ecological charge sheet includes the depletion of natural resources (especially water in the warm climates we like to visit); pollution, from atmospheric CO_2 to sewage, noise and ugly hotels; and physical impacts on ecosystems, for example giant cruise-ship anchors beating up sensitive coral reefs. For sure, the holiday industry is a crucial part of world trade, particularly important to many less well-off countries. But in reality, with as little as 22 per cent of tourism revenue ending up in local hands, more often than not wealth will not be distributed where it is needed.

Deep green:
Cycle-camping, or backpacking

Travel is the big environmental issue when it comes to holidays, particularly air travel, whose impacts are discussed in detail on p. 5 Even on other forms of public transport, your precious time off has some sort of carbon footprint. So to eliminate this completely, human power is the answer: and a bicycle, the most energy-efficient means of transport generally available, is the best way to translate this into a holiday. Camping helps to minimize the rest of your holiday's

impacts, because campers generally use relatively small amounts of water and fuel, minimal electricity and generate little waste. And because you can't do the trick, hated by local shopowners, of doing a vast supermarket shop and taking all your food with you, you'll be supporting the economy of your holiday destination too. If you are fortunate enough to live on the edge of somewhere beautiful, then taking off with just a rucksack is equally eco-friendly.

Dark green:
Fun at home

Unless your house is completely carbon-neutral (say a state-of-the-art eco-home or a yurt with a wood stove), or unless you camp in the garden, staying at home will always have more impact than an ultra-low-impact getaway like cycle-camping. You will inevitably use more water and electricity and will probably generate more waste. So it's not the greenest option; and it's possibly not too much fun either. Anyone wanting a deep green holiday that involves progress beyond the front door needs to get interested in tents and bicycles.

Quite green:
Pottering around on coaches, slow trains and boats for a 'do-it-yourself' holiday

The idea that staying close to home is the only way for your holiday to have a semblance of greenness is restrictive and simply untrue. A couple driving their powerful car to a second home in the country could, when the eco-reckoning is all done, be wreaking more havoc than people taking the train to a city break in Belgium. Using public transport (other than aeroplanes) is the best way to bring down the carbon cost of a holiday. Coaches are excellent in terms of fuel used per passenger kilometre, as are trains (unless they are of the high-speed variety, in which case their fuel consumption approaches that of aircraft; see trains, p. 260). Cargo ships offer the greenest option for long-haul travel (see boats, p. 46). When you finally reach your destination, staying with local people, patronizing local businesses and consuming at local levels is an infinitely better eco-bet than staying in monster resorts.

Light green:
Not too far in a fully loaded car

The travel impact of your holiday is, ultimately, all about pollution per passenger. In this respect, the traditional holiday-from-hell car packed with a quarrelling family and stuffed with luggage is not such a bad idea, as long as you don't drive it all the way to Phuket. Taking the example of a journey from London to Edinburgh, the car will get through, say, 60 litres of fuel, or about 12 litres per person. Over the same distance, a short-haul passenger jet will get through around 3,800 litres of jet fuel, about 30 litres per person if it has a full complement of passengers. To 'green up' such a car holiday, you could use the bikes you have brought along to do all the shopping and sightseeing trips once you have reached your destination, but this will clearly require a little bit of extra offsetting behaviour to counteract the miles-per-gallon reduction that a roofrack full of bicycles inevitably causes.

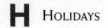

Not particularly green:
Holidays that involve flying

The vexed environmental issue of aviation is discussed in detail on p. 5. In summary: it may only account for 6 per cent of UK carbon emissions today, but it is growing fast: it is estimated that by 2012 there will be 12 million flights from the UK just to visit second homes. And it may only be around three times as bad in terms of fuel use per passenger kilometre than a car, but you can't drive a 3,500-kilometre round-trip for a long weekend, unless you take the term 'driving holiday' to its logical extreme. Nothing will crank up your carbon footprint faster than flying.

Not particularly green either:
Going on a cruise

If it's a sail-powered cruise on a boat made from FSC-certified wood, then clearly it would be higher up the green rankings. But most cruises are on dirty great big liners that burn vast tonnages of fuel, splurge huge quantities of waste into the oceans and fail to contribute anything but pollution to the beauty spots they visit. Even after new legislation has come into force for all cruise ships by 2010, they will still be able to dump hundreds of thousands of litres of untreated sewage (per ship) out at sea; and they will continue to emit large volumes of greywater (from washing, for example). And the fuel consumption of some liners is so great that they rival aeroplanes for litres per passenger kilometre.

Perhaps the least green thing it is humanly possible to do, ever:

Private jet to a desert golf resort

This ticks all the eco-devastation boxes. A private jet, preferably a really fast one tricked out to give maximum luxury to a minimum number of occupants, will create truly impressive amounts of atmospheric pollution per passenger. A golf resort will probably be owned by a multinational company and feed little into the local economy. Its water use will match the needs of 60,000 thirsty villagers, which will be extra-distasteful if the resort happens to be in a desert. And for good measure, the course will also need 1.5 tonnes of artificial fertilizers and pesticides to keep it in the condition that the jet-setting intercontinental golf-holidayer and all-round eco-hooligan has come to expect.

MORE INFORMATION
How to make long journeys by train: www.seat61.com

Jewellery

If you are worried about the impact on the environment of your decadent Western lifestyle, then fretting about your earrings is the least of your problems. Your choice of central-heating boiler, toilet or even lettuce will be of more concern to the planet than the tiny amounts of precious substances with which you may choose to adorn yourself. Whilst the extractive industries that wrest, say, gold and platinum from the ground are not without significant environmental issues, much of what they extract goes for industrial uses, so the relative contribution of jewellery is diminished. That said, the planet would doubtless be happier if we didn't keep blowing bits of it up and trickling noxious chemicals through the resulting rubble to extract precious materials.

Deep green:
Jewellery from renewable materials or certified producers with cast-iron environmental credentials

The most ascetic deep greenies would follow the lead of certain religious communities and simply shun all adornment, on account of its being entirely unnecessary. The energy spent crafting even the very eco-friendliest jewellery would be much more productively channelled into yurt maintenance, compost management or wind-turbine mechanics. However, for those who want to stay green but lighten up a little, there are many low-impact jewellery alternatives using renewable materials: wood, shells, acorns, even the odd animal tooth (assuming, of course, the latter has been retrieved in a humane and

148

sustainable manner). As a bonus, you don't have to make it all yourself to stay green: Fairtrade-certified items are easily available, offering a better deal for the producer and usually entailing low environmental impact. There is even a 'green standard' for gold (see below) that guarantees the metal's extraction has occurred without toxic chemicals and to strict ecological and social standards.

Dark green:
Second-hand jewellery

Following the argument that your purchase won't have directly stimulated any new environmental impacts, second-hand is a relatively green way to buy for most things, jewellery included.

Quite green:
Pearls

Completely natural pearls, which are formed inside molluscs such as mussels and oysters in response to an irritation, are very rare today, in part due to over-harvesting. Most contemporary pearls are 'cultured' by implanting a spherical irritation in a farmed mollusc, which then grows a pearl around it over time: when grown to the required size, the pearl is extracted. This doesn't necessarily represent a perfect lifestyle for the mollusc, but shellfish aquaculture is relatively eco-friendly, in that molluscs do not need unsustainable inputs of food; and as a bonus, their filter-feeding habits help to keep the water clean.

Pale green:
Silver and platinum

Both are products of highly resource-intensive mining operations but largely extracted as by-products of other metal mining: lead, copper or zinc in the case of silver; nickel in the case of platinum. Nickel in particular results in some quite impressive environmental impacts: smelters in the Russian city of Norilsk are said to account for one per cent of all global acid-rain-causing sulphur-dioxide emissions. However, since they are by-products, it is unfair to lay blame for such emissions at the door of silver and platinum, hence their relatively green position in this list.

Not particularly green:
Diamonds

Despite the fact that there is such a thing as the Council for Responsible Jewellery Practices, which aims to promote responsible social and environmental practice in the supply chain, it is hard to be completely comfortable about the impact of the diamond industry, particularly when it is run by a cartel. There are, of course, many issues around its social impact: for example the role diamonds have played in financing conflicts, or the hundreds of thousands of child or disadvantaged workers involved in diamond processing in India. Diamonds are extracted by the same kind of deep or open-pit mining methods as precious metals but do not use the same load of toxic chemicals as metals extraction.

Rarely green:
Gold

With the rich seams of gold that were once in them thar hills now all worked out, much gold mining involves blasting and pulverizing rock in open-pit mines and then extracting the gold using toxic chemicals such as cyanide solutions. In 'heap-leach' mining, the chemicals are allowed to trickle through huge mounds of ore in a process that produces 99.9 per cent waste, toxic mini-mountains and large amounts of liquid waste or 'tailings'. The most extreme metal-mining example must be the Mount Grasberg mine in Irian Jaya, Indonesia. Yielding copper as well as gold, when it is exhausted this mine will have resulted in the complete removal of a mountain, 3 billion tonnes of rock waste and a 230-square-kilometre hole in the jungle. There is such a thing as 'green gold' (see below), but most isn't.

MORE INFORMATION
'**Green**' **gold:** www.greengold-oroverde.org

Lamb and mutton

Sheep have the potential to produce the greenest meat of all. Intensive, indoor sheep-rearing is impossible: on the whole, sheep get to spend most of their lives outside, grazing naturally. In agricultural terms they convert land that is of marginal worth into valuable protein, wool and dairy products, enabling a living to be made in parts of the country that could not otherwise support agriculture. But the eco-friendliness of sheep is not a given. Whilst they can maintain certain ecosystems in a state that pleases everyone (chalk downlands, for example), they can wreck others, such as moorland, reducing biodiversity through over-grazing. The spring lambs of Easter can arrive at our table having had a somewhat unnatural start in life. And imported lamb raised in the most distant country from Britain has serious food-miles issues — or does it?

Deep green:
Hill lamb, in season

The main reason that meat has such a large impact on the environment is because of the huge amount of land needed to grow its feed and all the inputs of fuel, fertilizer and pesticides this usually needs. This makes meat very inefficient as a way of wresting human food from agricultural land and rightly allows vegetarians and vegans to feel ecologically self-righteous. Some sheep can get round this problem, though, by being sparsely stocked on high land that needs little or no artificial inputs. Hill lamb has probably the lowest impact of all, consisting of hardy breeds such as the Herdwick and

152

Swaledale, which, once weaned, enjoy a diet of fresh vegetation through the summer until they are ready for slaughter in late summer and autumn. The meat of such creatures is also available at other times of year in the form of mutton (aged two years or more) or hoggett (one to two years of age), so your purchase of relatively sustainable hill lamb is not restricted quite so narrowly. And there's always the freezer (see p. 122 for the relative eco-friendliness of these) if you need a guaranteed year-round supply of seasonal meat.

Dark green:
Organic lamb, in season

Not all hill lamb is organic, often because getting and keeping the prized certification is a costly business for a small operation running on thin margins. Much hill lamb will, however, match organic in environmental and animal-welfare terms. Buying organic does have a couple of environmental advantages, though, when you're looking beyond hill lamb. Because artificial fertilizers are not used, the animals are likely to be grazing on more natural and nutritious pasture, so the system can make for more tasty and nutritious meat – after all, sheep are what they eat – as well as saving the energy used in fertilizer manufacture. Overall, organic sheep farming has been shown to be over 30 per cent less energy-intensive than its conventional counterpart. Seeking out slower-growing traditional breeds, such as the Cheviot, Soay or Southdown, will also give a better eating experience.

Quite green:
New Zealand lamb

Stung by the impact of food-miles worries on its agricultural sector, New Zealand has hit back with a report claiming that much of its produce which so handily fills Britain's seasonal gap is, in fact, more climate-friendly. According to the report, New Zealand lamb is four times as energy-efficient as the UK product, even taking into account the shipping costs. This is because Kiwi lamb is produced with much less fertilizer and no concentrated feeds. Whilst the report illustrates that the food-miles issue is more complex than often characterized, it is also a little misleading. The most eco-friendly British lamb does not eat concentrates or graze on highly fertilized land and, of course, it does not need to make a 12,000-mile post-slaughter journey to market. But if the overall figures are to be believed, then even with the food miles New Zealand lamb makes a better bet environmentally than the average British product.

Not particularly green:
Spring lamb at Easter

Most breeds of sheep have a natural calendar which involves mating in the autumn, a winter gestation and birth in early spring, so that when young lambs are ready to be supplementing mothers' milk with fresh green grass, the grass is ready for them. This natural calendar would not, however, bring us fresh young lamb in time for Easter. That involves lambs being born unnaturally early in the dead of winter, living mostly indoors and being fed on grain-based 'concentrates' until it's time for the chop. So given the energy needed to make the feed, the heat and light – and also that the 'you are what you eat' factor means new-season Easter lamb won't be as tasty as the slower-grown, grass-fed animals – it's the least green lamby choice.

MORE INFORMATION
Listing of farmers' markets: www.farmersmarkets.net

Lawns

*I*s the greenest lawn the greenest lawn? It depends what it's made of and how it's kept that way. It's hard to take issue with lawns, which do many fine things for our environment as well as our social lives. They absorb some airborne pollutants and their roots play an active part in purifying the rain that soaks through them into groundwater. Unlike paving or decking, lawns stay cool when it's hot and they can play host to a surprising variety of flora and fauna. However, there is an ecological dark side to the manicured perfection of a British lawn, which relates in the main to how it is managed.

Deep green:
Wildflower meadow with the odd mown patch

Even the very smallest gardens can be major havens of biodiversity, particularly for invertebrates, of which hundreds – maybe even thousands – of species lurk in the soil, grass, plants and trees. However, a tightly clipped expanse of single-species lawn is limited in what it can do to encourage the bugs and butterflies that have largely been banished from much of the modern countryside by chemically managed monoculture crops. If you're prepared for a little untidiness, sowing the lawn with a mix of seeds that replicate a buzzing wildflower meadow will ultimately attract a much greater variety of species, many of them aesthetically pleasing and useful allies in any edible gardening efforts you may make. Such meadows will need no watering and only very occasional mowing, which, for maximum

156

eco-points, could be done in the old-fashioned way with a dirty great big scythe.

Dark green:
Home-grown, infrequently mown, unwatered lawn

Not everyone wants to wade through the tall grasses of a wildflower meadow. And much as lawns may be limited in the ecological services they can provide, they are infinitely better than the artificial alternatives as a base for your outdoor living. Growing your own is more of a faff than buying turf, but gets round all the issues of the turf business (see below). However, it is 'lawn care' that can really crank up the impact of your piece of green. Petrol mowers, for example, are not subject to the emissions regulations that govern cars and can kick out as much pollution in one hour as forty cars. A garden sprinkler can get through the average daily household water use for a family of four in thirty-six minutes. Less mowing is better for the lawn's health anyway: letting it grow to 4–5cm will help it to deal with dry periods better. And watering a lawn is completely unnecessary and done for purely aesthetic reasons. Grass is an incredibly tough plant and will bounce back even if it spends the latter half of the summer looking like desert scrub.

Quite green:
Buy turf

It is much easier to start with turf: your new lawn is ready for picnics in just a few days. The turf industry does have environmental impacts, though. The UK's biggest cultivator grows 3,500 acres of turf, a process which involves serious agricultural machinery, inputs of artificial fertilizer and then the fuel costs of transportation. Having said that, with the end product still undeniably green, buying turf remains infinitely preferable to the non-grass alternatives.

Pale green:
The perfect lawn

Impeccably manicured verdure, whilst still a living, natural organism with many positive qualities, has a high environmental cost. Keeping it green demands vast quantities of water in periods of dry weather. Top-dressings of fertilizer will be needed to keep it looking 'just so', as well as fungicides and selective herbicides to deal with disease and make sure that only one plant species is in charge. And then there's the incessant mowing which, if true perfection is to be achieved, will need to be done by one of the higher-end powered machines.

Not even a little bit green:
Artificial lawn

Could this be even less green than paving or decking? At least artificial grass offers decent drainage; and it won't need any of the eco-unfriendly inputs that a similarly pristine living lawn will need. However, it will need replacing after as little as fifteen years; it's made from fossil-fuel-derived products and it performs none of the CO_2 absorption, water purification, pollution absorption or wildlife habitat services that a real lawn will provide. Won't smell nice, either. So artificial grass's status as a big sheet of dead stuff in the middle of your garden condemns it to the least green spot.

Lighting

*L*ighting your home accounts, on average, for 3 per cent of your total energy use and about 16 per cent of your electricity bill, so at current prices it costs you a mere £70 a year (not including the price of the bulbs). Doing terrifically green and groovy things with the lights is not, therefore, going to save you vast amounts of money or the planet. But it's another of these actions that could have major effects if scaled up. An oft-quoted statistic is that a nationwide move to energy-saving light bulbs (which use around a quarter of the power of traditional incandescent bulbs) would enable us to lose a nuclear power station. Despite this tempting prospect – and the fact that low-energy lighting is becoming more affordable and casting a friendlier glow as compact fluorescent (CFL) bulbs improve – we are currently on track to increase our energy use from lighting significantly by 2020. This is because we've come a long way from the days when an overhead light and a couple of sturdy standard lamps were all we wanted to brighten the gloom of our living rooms. Today, we like designer light fittings with multiple spangly halogen spotlights – and it all adds up.

Deep green:
Darkness

Why add to the already serious problem of light pollution when you could live more in tune with nature's cycles? Darkness is nature's way of telling us to go to bed. Seekers after the deepest of green lifestyles will probably be off-grid and have their evenings centred around a campfire anyway, obviating the need for any more pesky, power-hungry and occasionally dangerous light sources.

Dark green:
Light-emitting diodes (LEDs)

Few of us want to go back to the Pleistocene darkness. The next greenest option is, ironically, the most high-tech: using lights based on LEDs. This lighting technology gets ecological brownie points for two reasons: the lights use very little power (typically 1–3 watts per bulb) and have an extremely long life, of up to 50,000 hours. All of which means they offer awesome energy savings even compared to CFLs (see below). This dark greenness comes at a price, though. LED bulbs cost more than CFLs but their main problem is the quality of light, which doesn't yet match the room-filling effect of fluorescents and incandescents. Watch this space, though: LEDs are developing fast and may soon become more practical for general household lighting.

Quite green:
Compact fluorescent bulbs (CFLs)

Until LEDs develop further, compact fluorescent light bulbs (CFLs) are the real-world option for low-energy lighting. CFLs typically use a quarter of the energy needed by incandescent bulbs to produce the same amount of light and they last as much as fifteen times longer. Anyone worried about the impact of their more complicated manu-facture (which takes four times more energy than is needed to make a 'normal' bulb) should be reassured that this is more than cancelled out by the energy savings. And fretters about mercury, which CFLs can contain, should also be comforted by the fact that the energy savings mean that less of it enters the environment overall, because of the reduction in fossil-fuel burning (which releases mercury). The downside of CFLs is that, unlike the sun or incandescent bulbs, they don't produce the 'full-spectrum' light we crave: but modern CFLs are a vast improvement on the stark glare of a standard fluorescent tube.

Not particularly green:
Incandescent lightbulbs

The writing is on the wall for Edison's invention. The reason the trusty traditional light bulb emits such a cosy warm glow is that most of what it is doing is creating heat, as its tungsten filament glows white-hot at 2,500°C. Only around 5 per cent of the energy it uses is turned into light. Banging the nail further into the incandescent bulb's coffin is the fact that it has a short life too (about 1,000 hours), so up to fifteen 100W bulbs are needed to give out the same light as a single 20W CFL. Fans of old-school bulbs could point out that the heat they kick out is not wasted, but contributes to domestic heating: however, light bulbs make an extremely inefficient heat source. Gas heating or better insulation compensates in a much more eco-friendly way for any missing heat.

Even less green:
Halogen spotlights

It's not that they necessarily use more power than incandescents (halogen spots are typically 50W), it's just that we like them in quantity.

A kitchen whose ceiling and cupboard undersides are studded with halogens, which is the fashion today, could easily be using up a not-so-cool 600W. Imagine two burly chaps at full pelt on exercise bikes in your kitchen to get an idea of how much energy this is. Thankfully, CFL technology is moving into this space, creating spotlights that run at just 7W each and don't need the bulky transformers that halogens demand. LED spots can provide directional light for even less, down to 1W.

Not even a little bit green:
Candles

Disappointing proof that traditional and old-fashioned doesn't always equal green. Candles end up here for several reasons. They are even less efficient at producing light than incandescents, with nearly all their energy turned into heat. Most are made from fossil-fuel-derived paraffin wax. And they kick out a noxious cocktail of pollutants directly into your home, particularly the craft-shoppe perfumed ones. I guess you could overcome the fossil-fuel issue by exclusively lighting your house with candles made of beeswax or beef tallow, but this is surely an option for extremist smallholders only.

MORE INFORMATION
Energy Saving Trust: www.est.org.uk
UK supplier of low-energy lightbulbs: www.megamanuk.com

Meat

(see also beef, p. 34; pork, bacon and ham, p. 204;
lamb, p. 152; chicken, p. 60)

*M*any green-minded types advocate abstinence as the only 'environmentally correct' response to meat-eating. There is no doubt that our carnivorous habits are having a staggering effect on the planet. It's all about inputs and outputs. The resources needed to create animal protein are enormous: it takes 54 calories of fuel energy to create one calorie of beef energy, for example; and each kilo of beef will additionally need 10 kilos of feed and 100,000 litres of water to produce. Farm animals account for 8 per cent of global human water use. As for outputs, nearly 20 per cent of global emissions of methane, a greenhouse gas 23 times more potent than CO_2, result from livestock flatulence. Overall, livestock contributes more to global warming than transportation. And intensive livestock farming is a major contributor to the eutrophication (over-enrichment) of ecosystems. But the problem is not meat-eating per se; it's the scale on which we practise it. Meat production has increased five-fold in the last fifty years: today, 75 per cent of agricultural land in the EU is given over to growing animal feed. If current trends continue, by 2050 livestock will be consuming as much food as the world's entire human population did in 1970. To say this is unsustainable is to stretch the power of understatement to breaking point. But livestock have a valuable part to play in agriculture. They add much-needed fertility, can produce resources from land that cannot support arable crops and can convert surpluses that would otherwise be wasted into usable food. And let's face it (if you're an omnivore), they taste mighty fine, have enormous food value and make an incalculable contribution to the quality of cuisine.

Deep green:

Sustainable quantities of wild meat, maybe roadkill

Any form of livestock agriculture has some kind of environmental impact (see also fish, p. 114). Truly wild meat, however, will have grown up in complete harmony with its surroundings and is also likely to have eaten a healthy diet, which will translate into tasty and nutritious meat. Much game, therefore, offers a sustainable meal for the green carnivore, albeit at a price and in season. Outside the game season, two creatures that are classed as vermin (and therefore fair game) are available all year round: step forward squirrels and wood-pigeon, both tasty and over-abundant. The confident and strong of stomach might want to investigate roadkill, which offers free protein for the hardcore forager.

Dark green:

Go veggie

Sadly for the carnivores among us, the planet would heave an enor-mous sigh of relief if we stopped eating farmed meat completely. Food takes up a big chunk of our environmental footprint – up to 40 per cent – and cutting out meat reduces this by the same amount. Without meat-eating, much of the 31 billion tonnes of livestock waste deposited on the planet each year would stop cluttering up the place and polluting the land, watersheds and atmosphere. Vast acreages of monocultural fodder crops, such as oilseed rape and maize, could be given over to cereals, pulses, vegetables and fruit for human consumption. And because some veggies are happy with animal products that don't result in the creatures' death – dairy products, eggs, honey – there would still need to be livestock, which would provide a source of much-needed fertility, essential for nutrient-hungry vegetable crops. In the real world, going veggie is arguably the greenest dietary choice. However, lacto-vegetarians must always bear in mind that dairy products mean that male animals will inevitably be born; and unless someone is going to run a vast live-stock sanctuary, with all the food and acreage it takes for these chaps to see out their natural lives, male calves, sheep and goats will have to be either shot at birth or eaten anyway.

Quite green:
Be a vegan

In theory, global veganism would be even better for the planet. A complete lack of farm-animal flatulence would clearly make for a happier atmosphere and, with livestock having no impact at all on the human food chain, there would be more for us to eat. However, with a lack of animal-derived fertility resulting in lower crop yields, the greater growing areas that would be necessary in 'vegan world' would mean less space for wildlife and biodiversity. And with apiculture now essential to the survival of the honeybee globally, vegans' aversion to honey could have dire consequences for the pollination of food crops.

Quite green 2:
Raise your own

If you want to appreciate (and manage) the environmental impact of meat, grow it yourself. To create happy pork, for example, you will need an area at least three times that of the average British garden just to keep two pigs in tolerably free-range conditions. They'll need plenty of fresh water and up to 3 kilos of high-protein, grain-based food a day, each. There are some advantages to this, though: you will never need to buy in any more compost for your veg patch, because pig manure is superb fertilizer. The meat will taste great, there will be no food miles (until you take them to slaughter, which can't legally happen in your back yard), all wastes will be recycled and you can't get much more 'traceable' than your own produce. However, the 'raise your own' option only really works for those of us with lots of land and either distant or very tolerant neighbours.

Light green:
Being a 'meat reducer', careful sourcing

This is the real-world option for non-veggies who want to be as green as possible. Why? Because sustainable mixed farming (which uses no fossil-fuel-derived inputs such as fertilizers and pesticides) will create a closed-loop system in which the animals are kept in symbiosis with the crops. Eat too much meat, and the system fails because you will be eating too much of a principal source of soil fertility (and also a potential source of other products, such as dairy, wool or eggs). This reflects what sustainable meat-eating would be like on a global scale: an occasional treat whose status reflects both its intrinsic value and the value of the time and resources that have gone into raising it. It's only when we try to subvert nature and produce meat intensively, for frequent, cheap consumption, that the environment suffers. Infrequent meat-eating also means that when you do buy meat, you can more easily afford to buy the best (see below).

Pale green:
Just careful sourcing

If you can't face bacon rationing, then buying meat that has the lightest environmental footprint is the next best choice. This doesn't mean slavishly seeking out organic produce, but it does mean avoiding any meat that is intensively farmed. This isn't a cheap choice: a once-happy chicken will cost four times as much as the cheapest, formerly miserable supermarket broiler. But given the food, water, land and effort needed to raise meat in a sustainable and humane way, cheap meat should always be viewed with intense suspicion. And, of course, there is a vast difference in eating quality between the best and worst meat. The best places for good meat are reputable butchers' shops (such as members of the Guild of Q Butchers), farmers' markets and farm shops; and buying direct from producers. Supermarkets are the home for most intensively farmed meat: here, the organic standard is the best guarantee of sustainability. The Red Tractor and Freedom Food badges, whilst they denote meat that is at least from the UK, can still be applied to intensively produced meat.

Not even a little bit green:
Lots of cheap meat and cheap, meaty ready meals

The welfare costs of cheap meat – sow stalls, veal crates, packed poultry sheds – are well documented. The environmental costs are less frequently discussed but becoming more and more pressing as production rises. As a general rule, what's bad for the animal or bird is also bad for the environment, and vice versa. Welfare standards in the UK are generally more rigorous than elsewhere in the world, where lighter regulation and more space can allow for intensive production on a truly biblical scale. The 7 million pigs of North Carolina, for example, produce more excrement and urine than the state's human inhabitants. If you've ever been downwind of an intensive pig or poultry operation, then you'll know about the airborne pollution, which contains methane, ammonia, nitrous oxide and particulates, but it's the land and watercourses that really suffer from intensive livestock farming, with overgrazing, pollution and damaged biodiversity just some of the impacts. Add to this the fuel costs of running high-tech indoor operations and the immense environmental costs, already discussed, of producing fodder crops on a large scale, and cheap meat costs an ecological fortune. So buying lots of it is the least green dietary decision you can make. To make it worse, buying it in ready meals means even more energy and packaging, plus the fact that even a ready meal labelled British could contain meat from anywhere in the world.

MORE INFORMATION
Guild of Q Butchers: www.guildofqbutchers.com
'Livestock's long shadow': detailed report into the
environmental impact of livestock via www.fao.org

Media (news)

*D*ead trees bad, Internet good. At least that's the intuitive response to the question of what is the greenest news medium. But it ignores a couple of crucial facts that are often overlooked. The first is that trees are a crop, a renewable resource. (Admittedly one that has been created by felling old-growth forest to replace it with intensively managed monoculture plantations.) The dead trees in your newspaper will soon be replaced by new ones. And the 'Internet good' assumption forgets the quite staggering power demands of the infrastructure needed to put a web page in your face. The monster server arrays that run the Internet suck down power and then demand gigawatt-hungry aircon systems to keep them cool. So the green media landscape is not quite as predictable as it might seem.

Deep green:
Disconnection

Aaaah, bliss! Relief from the constant search for a news fix is matched by the satisfaction of knowing your media habits no longer have an environmental footprint. As a fully fledged deep greenie, the only news that matters will concern events on your smallholding; and this can be gathered directly by you or other members of the community. Even weather forecasting can be managed in the traditional way with pine cones, dowsing and divination.

Dark green:
Radio, preferably wind-up

A wind-up radio means you can access media from all around the world with no need for any electricity infrastructure at all, making this the perfect option for the deep greenie who secretly yearns to know what is happening beyond the wattle-and-daub walls of the small-holding. Even plugged in to the mains, radios use very little electricity compared with other media devices – a mere few watts. And whilst it is difficult to arrive at exact figures, it is fair to assume that the per-person share of the global radio network's power demands is far lower than for other, hungrier media.

Quite green:
Television

How green this is does rather depend on the telly (see p. 247 for the relative greenness of these). But taking an average figure of, say, 150W per television, the analogue network's annual power consumption of 239GWh, the UK's 26 million tellies and allowing for 30 minutes of news viewing per day per TV, we arrive at an annual per-TV figure of 38.4kWh, which compares favourably in both power and carbon terms with both Internet-based news and newspapers.

Light green:
Newspapers

'Old media' doesn't get consigned to un-green history just yet. A study by the Carbon Trust, which looked at every aspect of newspaper production from tree-felling to distribution, calculated that a copy of the *Daily Mirror* results in 174 grams of CO_2 emissions. This is more than three times as much as half an hour of goggling at the TV news, but better, surprisingly, than a similar amount of time spent surfing news websites. Clearly there is massive variation in the eco-footprint of publishing. It depends on everything from the energy mix of the paper-producing country's electricity supply (Sweden's, for example, has a high percentage of low-carbon hydroelectricity) to the amount of recycled paper involved (the newspaper industry average is 70 per cent) to the fuel efficiency of delivery lorries. Perhaps surprisingly, delivery of heavy newspapers accounts for only a small percentage of their overall footprint: paper manufacture is by far the most energy-intensive activity, followed by printing and disposal.

Pale green:
The Internet

Putting new media, traditionally seen as a paragon of low-resource greenness, below newspapers in the ranking might seem contentious. And it probably is, given that a truly representative calculation of relative environmental impact is difficult to arrive at. However, the fact that the Internet consumes a great deal of electricity cannot be denied. A study conducted in early 2007 estimates that the total power use of the servers that run the Internet and their associated cooling and auxiliary services runs to about 170 billion kWh per year. Allocate this evenly to the world's 1 billion Internet users and each is therefore responsible for 170kWh of power per year, which dwarfs the 30kWh per year that your average PC and router will use in half an hour of daily news browsing. Put the two together and the carbon footprint of a daily rootle around for news on the web weighs in at 234.7 grams of CO_2 per day, which makes the *Daily Mirror* a better bet, if only in environmental terms.

Not particularly green:
Magazines

Back to normal: things that are fun being classified as un-green. The production and printing of glossy magazines takes more energy than newspapers and they are heavier, slightly harder to recycle and can't easily be composted (a great way of getting rid of newspapers, which sort out the carbon/nitrogen balance in a compost heap).

Not even a little bit green:
A nationwide network of town criers

Sometimes the oldest-fashioned ways of doing things are the least eco-friendly (see also lighting, washing dishes). Perhaps unsurprisingly, no one has as yet done a complete 'life cycle analysis' of the environmental impact of a return to the widespread use of stentorian gentlemen to deliver the news. But given the size of modern populations and today's 24-hour news cycle, it is a safe bet that the sheer number of criers and the infrastructure needed to put them within earshot of the entire population would create a quite unacceptable environmental burden.

Milk

Can milk be green? It's a tough one. Livestock farming (see also meat, p. 163) has an enormous environmental impact at the scale on which it is currently practised. Thanks largely to the fact that the average dairy cow emits an impressive 32+kg per day of the potent greenhouse gas methane, milk and dairy products account for 5 per cent of all 'global warming potential' in the EU. And because of the runoff of fertilizers, manure and slurry, the milk industry also contributes significantly to the eutrophication (over-enrichment) of rivers, lakes and streams. On a small, mixed farm, dairy cattle and their outputs (offspring, manure) can be integrated into the farming enterprise. But dairy farming in the UK is intensifying, resulting in fewer, larger farms, and such operations have greater localized pollution potential. Then there's the whole 'what happens to the calves' issue that so vexes those concerned with animal welfare. To produce milk, a cow must have a calf; as a result, intensive dairy farming results in many unwanted male calves that may be exported live to indoor veal farms or simply killed. So getting a truly green pinta is a tricky business. As with so many animal-related dietary issues, abstinence is the greenest option; but there are relatively eco-friendly options for milk drinkers too.

Deep green:
Unpasteurized (raw) milk

Apologies to readers in Scotland, where the sale of unpasteurized or 'raw' cows' milk is illegal. Why is 'green top' milk so green?

Pasteurization, which was introduced to kill pathogens and prolong shelf-life, also knocks out some of the vitamins in milk, denatures its proteins and makes it harder to digest. A vigorous debate rages about this issue, with food authorities generally lobbying for a ban (in order to eliminate any health risk) whilst raw-milk devotees point to both anecdotal and research-based evidence of its health benefits. Raw milk can only be sold at the farm gate or in a farmhouse catering operation, or via a milk round, both of which are pretty low-impact distribution methods (as long as you don't drive 50 miles to the farm to get your milk). Add to this the facts that the majority of raw-milk producers will be small-scale farms with a relatively low or even positive environmental impact and that vast volumes of milk don't have to be heated up in the pasteurization process, and going raw is a good way to get green milk. Keeping your own cow gives you even more control over the greenness of your milk, but it is a complex business suitable for committed small-scale farmers only. The scarcity of raw milk means you will inevitably become a 'milk reducer' too, which is no bad thing for the planet given the impact of dairy farming when practised on a large scale.

Dark green:
Organic milk and less of it

Organic milk production is not all ecological loveliness. Yes, the cattle have a 95 per cent organic diet that studies have suggested results in a healthier end product. However, if all of the UK's dairy herd were organic it would need more space and create, potentially, more greenhouse gases because the lower milk yields of organic cows mean that more animals would be needed to create the same amount of milk. Hence more methane emissions per litre. This touches on a core issue in livestock farming. You can reduce some environmental issues by farming more intensively, but in doing so you create others. Some of these are environmental: the use of more machinery, more artificial fertilizer, more intensively farmed animal feed and the creation of concentrated pollution. Others have to do with animal welfare: the exhausted, high-yield dairy cow, the short-lived intensive broiler chicken. Organic production has fewer of these 'externalities', so drinking organic milk but less of it seems like the next best choice after raw.

Quite green:
Modest amounts of milk from the milkman

The gentle electric whine and clink of a milk float in the wee small hours may be a less common sound these days, but doorstep delivery is still a possibility for many. The milkman gets green brownie points for two main reasons: a single electric vehicle delivering to many houses is better in energy terms than many cars trundling down to the local shop; and glass bottles, whilst much more energy-intensive to produce than alternatives, can be re-used many times and then recycled easily, unlike the cartons in which much milk is currently packaged. Organic milk in glass bottles is also available from some firms.

Pale green:
Goat's milk

Producers point to the health benefits of goat's milk, suggesting that with a protein structure more closely allied to human milk it is easier to digest and good for those with an intolerance to cow's milk. Goat farming happens on a small scale so its impact is relatively light; however, producers tend not to be fully organic because the animals spend more time indoors than organic standards demand.

Not particularly green:
Any old milk

Any old milk from the shop down the road will probably come from intensively farmed cows that spend much more time indoors than they would like and have been fed on concentrated feeds that do not reflect their natural diet of fresh grass. It's worth remembering at this point that the adage 'you are what you eat' applies to milk as well as meat. The quality of cow's milk reflects what the cow eats and the milk of grass-fed cows has, among other things, higher levels of essential fatty acids that are lacking in Western diets. Ironically, these are now added back into intensively farmed milk by putting flaxseed and fish-oil supplements into the animals' feed. Sterilized milk has been more severely heated for a long life in a process that also adversely affects its nutrient content. And skimmed milk? Obtaining a valuable product from livestock at great cost to the animal and the environment then removing its very essence seems to defy all reason.

Not even a little bit green:
Soya milk

It lines the shelves of wholefood shops in both conventionally farmed and organic forms, offering a milky alternative to those for whom the whole dairy trip is a little too heavy. But can soya milk be green, given that on current projections the cultivation of soya beans will have destroyed a UK-sized chunk of South American forests and savannah by 2020? Soya cultivation is associated with vast monocultures and widespread use of GM technology. The brands that hang out in health shops are at pains to stress that their beans have a less environmentally destructive genesis. But they don't mention health concerns over the plant oestrogens in soya products that are processed by modern methods. Those looking to avoid dairy altogether can find the calcium they need less controversially, from leafy vegetables and nuts.

MORE INFORMATION
Find out if there is a milk round near you:
www.findmeamilkman.net

Motorcycles

Motorcycles are not, on the face of it, terribly green things. Their association is often with reckless speed, loud noise and visible emissions, none of which is a typical characteristic of eco-friendliness. That said, much has changed since the greasy, smoky mods-and-rockers era, which for many is still the reference point for motorcycling. Most bikes, even absurdly fast ones, consume less fuel than cars and their emissions are improving rapidly and rarely create clouds of noxious smoke. And thanks to their relative scarcity – motorcycles account for only one per cent of annual British vehicle kilometres – their overall contribution to the country's megatonnage of atmospheric pollution is very small.

Deep green:
Ride a bicycle, for goodness' sake!

No self-respecting deep greenie is going to be seen riding a motorcycle. They're far too much fun, for a start, and we can't be having too much of that in our quest to save the planet overnight. Motorcycles are also very impractical: a tandem can carry the same amount of people and luggage, albeit not at the same speeds, but with no pollution and presenting much less danger to the jaywalking public. And the older motorcycles likely to be in the price bracket of the frugal deep greens among us will not have been subject to today's more stringent emissions legislation and will therefore have much higher levels of poisonous carbon monoxide and hydrocarbon emissions than most cars.

Dark green:
Electric scooter

There's one just about to come on the market at the time of writing. The Vectrix is subject to the usual electric vehicle range restrictions, with its maximum 68 miles between charges dropping to a mere 25 miles if you wind it up to its maximum speed of 62 m.p.h. Then you'll need an extended break in a greasy caff that's generous enough to let you plug in for the couple of hours it takes to charge it back up again. With a 1.5kW charger, this does make for cheap mileage and low (around 16g/km) CO_2 emissions from the electricity used. Such short range, however, confines the electric scooter to commuting and urban pottering duties, where its near £7,000 price tag and £2,000 battery pack (which will eventually need to be replaced) make it a very costly way to save the planet on two wheels.

Quite green:
Just doing track days

Why bother riding a motorcycle on the road? Modern machines can exceed the national speed limit in first gear and opening the throttle to any significant degree can get you into legal and/or mortal bother very quickly indeed. Racetracks are safer and a great deal more fun. Once you've passed your test (on a hired bike), simply book some days at 'race school' where you will be able to hare around as fast as you like. The time and cost involved will mean you inevitably do a much lower mileage than a motorcycle owner, so you can feel (relatively) smug about the eco-friendly side of things as well as having no worries about insurance, theft, servicing costs, speed cameras or high-speed encounters with drystone walls.

Light green:
Diesel motorcycle

This is very much a minority pursuit at the moment, and for good reason: in a world that loves speed and relishes a fine engine note, diesel motorcycles are distinctly sluggish and make an unappealing racket. They do, however, offer outstanding fuel economy (up to 200 m.p.g.), good reliability and could, if the owner wished, be run on vegetable oil (see p. 56), making their mileage entirely carbon-neutral. There are more modern diesel prototypes currently in development that will offer less humiliating performance for still excellent fuel economy.

Pale green:
Weedy moped, two-up

Sadly for any snarling petrolheads who also have a nagging green conscience, automotive environmental devastation is partly a function of horsepower. The more 'grunt' your bike has, the more greenhouse gas it's going to kick out. And unless it has a side-car, which is likely to damage your image as well as your fuel consumption, a bike can't reduce its per-person environmental impact by a factor of more than two. However, cheap, simple 50cc mopeds can offer fuel consumption of over 100 m.p.g., twice as good as even a frugal car. So even accounting for the weight of your pillion you could get emissions down almost to the same per-capita level as a Prius full of people, without all the high technology and expense.

Not even a little bit green:
Gas-turbine motorcycle

Even at the very top of the motorcycle performance tree, things are still relatively economical. Ultra-fast sportsbikes such as the Yamaha YZF-R1 can turn in 40 m.p.g. or so if not ridden too hard: you won't get that from the Porsche or Ferrari you'll need to achieve the same speed. Those bent on environmental devastation with their bikes need to try harder and spend a bit more. The answer is the MTT Turbine Superbike, which is powered by a gas-turbine helicopter engine modified to run on diesel. Holding world records as the most powerful and expensive production motorcycle, this awesome machine will top 200 m.p.h., scare the living daylights out of you and return 4–6 m.p.g., worse than a large lorry.

Not even a little bit green either:
'Overlanding'

Given their rarity, an unsettling (if thrilling) riding experience and rather short range, it is unlikely that the planet is going to be too irritated by gas-turbine motorcycles. Greenness is ultimately a function of mileage rather than horsepower: 50,000 miles on an old knocker is much worse than the odd weekend blast on your cherished trophy sportsbike. So despite the rugged frontier spirit of it all, the chaps who head off round the world for a two-wheeled gap year are arguably wreaking more eco-havoc with the 7-odd tonnes of CO_2 they will emit than the 'born-again' bikers hurling themselves into hedges of a sunny Sunday afternoon.

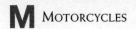

More Information
The Tandem Club of Great Britain: www.tandem-club.org.uk
Vectrix Electric Scooters: www.zevltd.com
List of UK track days: www.biketrackdays.co.uk

Oils (edible)

'Oil crops' form a huge part of world agriculture, yet only a tiny proportion of them end up in bottles in our kitchens. The massive increases in rapeseed, palm and soybean oil growing in the last few decades are mainly down to the demands of the food-processing and livestock-feed industries and, increasingly, the biofuel business (see p. 56). Most of the EU's oilseed rape crop, for example, ends up in fuel tanks rather than stomachs these days. So in the great green scheme of things, changing what goes into the salad bowl or frying pan isn't going to save the planet overnight. But as with all foods, there are 'high-impact' and 'low-impact' choices, and some shades in between.

Deep green:
Cold-pressed, single-producer, organic, extra-virgin olive oil

Olive oil isn't all ecological loveliness. Increasingly, especially in southern Spain, it is grown intensively, at unsustainable densities of up to 1,000 trees per hectare, 5–10 times the traditional norm. However, on a smaller scale olive oil is relatively ecologically benign. As a perennial tree crop, it does not need fields to be dug up and replanted every year like many of the other main oil crops. Cold pressing does need machinery, but not the heat or chemicals with which oils can be extracted. Unless it is badged as being 'produced and bottled by' the same person, or from a particular region or a named grower, even the poshest-looking oil could be a blend of oils that have travelled from all over the place. So 'single-producer'

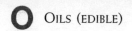

labelling is the best bet for quality and food miles. Organic standards will mean that the trees have been tended with biodiversity and sustainability in mind. And extra-virgin oils are of the highest quality, with the lowest acid content.

Dark green:
Cold-pressed, organic rapeseed oil

The oil from this turnip-related plant has only been edible to humans relatively recently, as strains were bred in the twentieth century that had lower levels of a toxic acid. Despite blanketing – some would say blighting – the countryside of Britain and other temperate countries with its vivid yellow flowers thanks to its suitability as a livestock feed and biofuel crop it gets green points as an edible oil for several reasons. With cold pressing, its processing is reasonably energy-efficient and the solid by-product goes off to make animal feed. It can be grown locally, minimizing food miles; its flowers make superb forage for bees and, as a result, honey can also be a by-product. Rapeseed oil also offers a higher omega-3 content than almost any other oil apart from linseed, which makes it a healthy choice too. Organic production, as with olive oil, is kinder to the environment and needs no energy-intensive agrochemicals.

Light green:
Organic sunflower oil

Those lovely, picturesque fields of sunflowers that carpet France are not, mostly, going to make it into lovely, picturesque, rustic gourmet meals. Mostly they will be turned into animal feed and oils used in processed food, as well as being sold as domestic cooking oil. Sunflower has a relatively low yield per hectare and growing it demands plenty of artificial fertilizer and pesticides, so organic is the best bet from an energy and environmental point of view.

Not particularly green:
Any old veg oil

Move away from the lovely but costly world of cold-pressed oils and the greenness fades away. It is more efficient, and cheaper, to extract oil from oil crops by heating or with solvent extracts: these can simultaneously remove the goodness from oil and crank up its ecological footprint. Any old veg oil may also have been bleached and deodorized, adding more energy to the production process.

Not even a little bit green:
Palm oil

You won't see this in British shops, at least not bottled for cooking. It is high in unhealthy saturated fats and mostly used for industrial purposes; however, it does end up in many processed foods. Demand for palm oil, which offers a high yield in relation to cooler-climate vegetable oils, can result in rainforest destruction as the forests are cleared for big, monocultural plantations. The best way to avoid it is to stay away from processed food.

Oranges and orange juice

Yes, they come from afar; but oranges don't fly, so the emissions per fruit are not enormous. Orange cultivation, however, can hit the environment fairly hard, depending on where and how they are grown. In 'conventional' systems, oranges are dosed with large quantities of artificial fertilizer and even more pesticides than pesticide-sodden bananas (see p. 20), meaning lots of energy use and direct environmental pollution, as well as residues in the fruit. And in countries where they need to be irrigated, oranges guzzle a staggering 9 million litres of water per hectare per year. As a result of this water use and the fuel needed in the juicing process, it has been estimated that ten glasses of orange juice account for 10,000 glasses of water and one glass of crude oil.

Deep green:
Apples

If you're being a purist – and anyone in this category most definitely is – then oranges are an unnecessary, decadent indulgence. Never mind the environmental impact of growing them, all that trucking and shipping is entirely unnecessary if you can manage through the year on fresh, dried and even frozen versions of things that grow locally. Eschewing oranges may remove a flash of colour from your life and diet, but just think of the rising sea lapping up to your organic flower beds and bite into a wizened old stored apple instead.

Dark green:
Organic oranges at any time of year

Our nearest oranges, those of the southern Mediterranean, have a season which runs from November to May, with a couple of short but memorable special events in the shape of Seville oranges in January and February and blood oranges in February and March. Outside these months, our suppliers switch to antipodean oranges, whose season, which runs from April to October, neatly fills the gap. Oranges from South Africa or Argentina may be seven times further away than those that have rumbled up the autoroute from Spain, but shipping uses ten times less energy per tonne/kilometre than road freight, so the food miles are comparable in terms of the emissions they cause. Organic oranges are grown in systems which are better for biodiversity and soil fertility; copper-based fungicides are used, but in limited amounts.

Quite green:
Orange juice from concentrate

Here's a controversial placing for something that has a bad rep as an industrial bulk commodity. Concentrate is obtained by evaporating the water from orange juice; the resulting product is then stored at −12°C. Why is it in any way green? FCOJ (frozen concentrated orange juice) has six times less volume than the fresh stuff and is reconstituted in the country where it is to be sold, so the energy needed for shipping is much lower. Still, this advantage may well be eroded by the energy needed to remove and then replace the water and for refrigeration; but if the juice is of Brazilian origin (much is) there is a chance it will not have been irrigated, providing a balancing ecological advantage.

Light green:
Freshly squeezed orange juice

It certainly tastes better and it beats 'not from concentrate' (NFC) – which usually comes between freshly squeezed and FCOJ in the perceived quality stakes – on environmental grounds too. Shipping volumes for freshly squeezed juice will be higher than for NFC, as the whole fruit is imported and squeezed locally. But unlike NFC it doesn't need energy-intensive pasteurization and if it's from organic oranges, then the overall impact will be relatively low.

Not particularly green:
Any old orange

Orange cultivation is going the way of so many agricultural commodities: bigger farms, less labour, more fertilizers and pesticides. The latter are a particular issue with oranges: in recent tests, all oranges sampled had pesticide residues, with nearly 90 per cent having multiple residues. These are contained largely in the skin and are said to pose no health risk. However, the energy needed to make and deliver fertilizers and pesticides adds significantly to an orange's ecological footprint, as do the residues left in the local environment.

Not even a little bit green:
Orange juice 'drinks'

Now you could argue that because they contain as little as 5 per cent juice, such drinks make economical use of a valuable agricultural commodity. But most orange juice 'drinks' also contain copious sugar or artificial sweeteners and a host of industrially produced additives. Add to this the often lurid and complex packaging, with its embodied energy, toxicity and waste issues and such 'drinks' earn their place in the least green slot.

Orange season

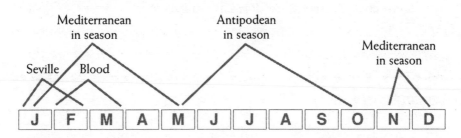

Pasta

*D*iffering relative environmental impacts in pasta? Yes: even this humble staple has a few shades of green, albeit not scientifically defined. Discounting non-wheat pastas (rice, millet) aimed at the gluten-intolerant, the main differences in conventional pasta's eco-friendliness depend on how its core ingredient is grown and what sort of pasta is at issue.

Deep green:
Organic dried pasta

Dried pasta is made from 'hard' durum wheat whose high gluten content means that the simple addition of water creates a dough that can be moulded and extruded into many fantastic shapes. So having just two simple, natural ingredients gives dried pasta a generally high eco-rating. Durum wheat is generally grown in warmer climates than our own, so local dried pasta is unlikely to be on the shelves, meaning some food miles are inevitably involved. However, organic pasta will have taken less energy to grow because of the lack of artificial fertilizer and agrochemicals needed for the wheat. In an energy study of dried pasta, its cooking accounted for half of all the energy expenditure for which it is responsible, so boiling your pasta in the most eco-friendly way possible (see cookers, p. 86) will shrink your pasta's carbon footprint.

Dark green:

Your own home-made fresh pasta, made with the most 'right-on' ingredients possible

It doesn't get more achingly middle-class than this. But in the absence of a superb Italian deli, making your own is the only way to achieve silky fresh-pasta nirvana. Fresh pasta gets knocked off the eco top spot because it needs eggs, which come with their own ecological cost (see eggs, p. 104), so the key to virtuous home-made pasta is careful sourcing. Which means eggs from your own hens or from birds that have otherwise lived the high life. This will cost more but will have the added benefit of creating much better pasta. Organic flour will have had a lower environmental cost, and the whole home-made thing cuts down on food miles and eliminates packaging. And the hand-cranked production process is nice and eco-friendly too.

Quite green:

Conventional dried pasta

Even if its main ingredient is not grown organically, dried pasta remains one of the least mucked-about-with processed foods. Whilst conventional wheat is grown with plenty of pesticides and herbicides, few residues are reported in the finished product. If your food concerns include the ethical as well as the environmental, then it's worth bearing in mind that the UK's leading brand Buitoni is owned by Nestlé, whose activities in marketing breastmilk substitutes have led to many boycotts of their products, despite the company's refutation of campaigners' claims.

Pale green:
Vacuum-packed 'fresh' pasta

Even with its shorter cooking time, the fresh stuff lost out to dried pasta in an environmental impact study because of the extra energy needed to produce the eggs and refrigerate the finished product. The packaged 'fresh' pasta that packs supermarket shelves is pasteurized and vacuum-packed for a long shelf-life; and unless the label explicitly says otherwise, its fillings and extra ingredients may not come from the most eco-friendly of sources (eggs from caged hens, for example).

Peas

The pea and its environmental impact are the focus of much study. In a paper with the clearly irresistible title 'Give peas a chance', academics, identifying peas as 'the example of a Fordist production and consumption system', examine the social and technical sustainability of the pea business. Unilever, owner of Birds Eye Walls, which sells 50 per cent of the UK's frozen peas, is involved in a project entitled 'In pursuit of the sustainable pea'. Phew. Just what is it that makes this small green family favourite the focus of such intellectual firepower? It's a combination of peas' popularity and the fact that much technology is needed to ensure a year-round supply of a very seasonal product whose quality degrades rapidly after picking. So picking the greenest pea is not without its complexities.

Deep green:
Grow your own

It's not that hard to grow the odd pea, but you will need a fair bit of space to get a decent crop. Peas fix nitrogen in the soil and thus contribute fertility to your garden, but a season of wrestling with the weeds, pests and diseases with which they compete will give you new-found respect for commercial growers, particularly those who try to do it organically. Nothing will ever taste better than peas straight off the vine, because the sugars in peas start turning to starch immediately after they are picked. However, your pea supply will be limited to a seasonal window of about May to August; thereafter it's either pea abstinence, freezing or drying your own crop (assuming

193

you grew enough to do this in the first place) or, more sensibly, buying frozen peas.

Dark green:
Local peas in season

Fresh peas in season will have made it to the shops without any need for the energy-intensive blanching, freezing and packaging that their year-round frozen cousins endure. A downside, however, is that unless they have been rushed from field to shop in double-quick time, they may well be less tasty and nutritious than the frozen variety, whose nutrients are locked in by freezing within just a few hours of picking. So if you are lucky enough to have good greengrocers or farmers' markets nearby, their 'plot to plate' distance – which is likely to be shorter than a supermarket's – will get you a tastier and fresher pea.

Quite green:
Frozen peas

It's true that the process of growing and freezing peas is highly indus-trialized. Crops are treated with herbicides and insecticides, residues of which made it into 36 per cent of samples the last time peas were tested. The pea fields are hardly havens of biodiversity; and the fuel-guzzling process of harvesting with large, specialized machines and then blanching and blast-freezing the crop uses yet more energy. However, at least the British frozen-pea industry is largely local, with relatively low food miles. Because organic production is tricky, producers are looking at other ways to reduce the impact of the crop and achieve a 'sustainable' pea.

Quite green 2:
Organic frozen peas

With just 160 hectares of organic peas in Britain, it is almost certain that any you find in the shops will have been imported. They are unlikely to have been air-freighted, so the impact of food miles will not be so severe. However, as no empirical analysis exists of the overall environmental impact of organic imported frozen peas vs conventional local ones, they get equal billing with the great British frozen pea.

Pale green:
Tinned peas

Equally, no analysis exists of the relative impact of tinned vs frozen peas. But the energy needed to manufacture the tins, combined with their extra weight, adds to their environmental burden. And in terms of nutrition, one can at least draw an inference from the fact that the canned-food industry makes favourable comparisons with fresh peas but neglects to pit tinned against frozen.

Not even a little bit green:
Air-freighted fresh peas

It is an inescapable fact of seasonality that we have to do without local fresh peas for about seven months of the year. Keen, as always, to seek competitive advantage from offering the widest possible range of fresh stuff, retailers look far overseas to keep the shelves green and fresh. All imported fresh peas are air-freighted and they are fourth in a list of polluting food imports, being responsible for 45,000 tonnes of CO_2 emissions per year. It takes around two and a half times the energy to get them from plot to plate as it does with local produce. And the longer journey time means they will never have the nutritional value of frozen peas. So the 'strong green' view is that importing what is essentially a luxury crop with a perfectly good, less energy-intensive frozen substitute is entirely environmentally irresponsible. Detractors may point out that such long-distance agriculture injects vital funds into developing countries; but in practice, the funds often end up concentrated in a few hands. There are surely better ways to boost developing economies than with such ecologically destructive trade.

Pea season

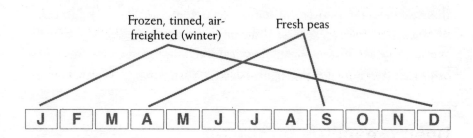

Frozen, tinned, air-freighted (winter)

Fresh peas

J F M A M J J A S O N D

Pets

Surely pets – usually friendly, sometimes cute, often furry and/or fluffy – are eco-friendly? Not a bit of it. Creatures in their natural environments are fine, because ideally the natural predator/prey balance keeps things in check: once there are no more mice to eat, the cats die off, then the mice bounce back, the cats return and so it goes on. As soon as we start looking after animals, though, we give them a hugely unfair advantage, cosseting them to often ludicrous degrees so they can go off and wreak havoc on the biosphere with impunity. Many pets, like most humans, are net consumers of natural resources, adding nothing back (or in the case of cat and dog faeces, adding it back in all the wrong places). It is said that the average British dog is better fed than the average human in the poorest 20 per cent of the world. Of course the difficult calculation is what humans would do if deprived of their favourite pets: studies suggest they would be more of a burden on the health service and possibly grumpier too: illness and anger can both have negative environmental consequences, from the need to manufacture more medicines to global thermonuclear conflict. So there is by definition a bit of subjectivity in the pet ranking that follows.

Deep green:
Garden wildlife and pond life

This is pet ownership without the ownership. Manage your garden or outside space for wildlife and before long there could potentially be a vast range of fauna for you to interact with, from invertebrates to birds and small mammals. Wildlife gardening, which involves strategic untidiness, the creation of encouraging habitats such as ponds and the growing of plants and shrubs that provide food and shelter, means any financial outlay will be minimal. You'll get a range of different 'pets' through the year, which has got to be more interesting than just looking at the same old budgie day in, day out. And most importantly, you will be contributing to Britain's biodiversity, which is being assailed on all sides by intensive agriculture, habitat depletion, climate change and – to an extent – other pets.

Deep green 2:
Honeybees

Not very cute, admittedly. But you do get to be in charge of them, as much as one is ever in charge of another species. Honeybees play a vitally important role in pollinating plants and trees and are currently threatened by a disease, introduced from overseas, against which they have no natural defence; at the time of writing they are suffering profound population crashes around the world. Unless we keep up, or preferably step up, our beekeeping activities, honeybees will die out. So keeping them as 'pets' is good from an environmental point of view; and of course you get the added benefit of honey – as much as 40 kilos per year from a single hive. Carefully sited, one or two beehives can exist perfectly safely in even the smallest of gardens.

Dark green:
Herbivorous outdoor fish

Indoor aquaria can guzzle electricity, maybe 400kWh per year and upwards. Plus the fish need feeding. Choose herbivorous fish like carp and put them in an outside pond, though, and they'll need virtually no inputs of food or resources. And when you're bored of watching them swim around, you can eat them. Perfectly green.

Quite green:
Chickens

Hens are almost cute and definitely have personalities, giving them more 'pet value' than the choices thus far. They do need some inputs of grain-based feed, which gives them an environmental cost, but they'll also eat your veg scraps, thus performing a useful recycling role. Most importantly, though, they produce extremely useful by-products of eggs and manure, helping to reduce your family's overall eco-footprint. No problem with disposal of your aged hens either: long, slow cooking should do the trick.

Pale green:
Rabbits

Rabbits can destroy a vegetable plot in double-quick time and, even after they've done that, are likely to need bought-in food. However, they are the only truly cute pet that is also usefully edible, and as such just make it on to the green scale. Whether this eco-advantage of rabbits will find favour with the whole family is of course a moot point.

Pale green 2:
Pigs (see also pork, p. 204)

Highly intelligent, gregarious and friendly, pigs can be an excellent addition to the family, as long as the family accepts that the pig's time is short. Pigs do consume a great deal of high-protein food, the growing of which carries a high environmental cost. However, in return they provide generous helpings of fertility to the garden (which will need to be extremely large) as well as companionship and, of course, many excellent meals.

Not even a little bit green:
Cats and dogs

To get an idea of the environmental position of cats and dogs, it's instructive to start by looking at inputs and outputs. Britain's dogs alone, for example, consume 765,000 tonnes of food a year, which is converted annually into 365,000 tonnes of excrement, one billion litres of urine and a whole lot of barking. Our cats get through 425,000 tonnes of food per year and because this is clearly not enough, they also kill 220 million small animals and 55 million birds. Thanks to the concrete with which many canine and feline habitats are paved, many of the animals' outputs get washed into watercourses where they have an adverse impact on aquatic ecosystems. Even if cats can be persuaded to 'go' in a specific place, their litter, unless it is of an eco-friendly type, does not rot down and the deeply unpleasant parasites in their faeces can persist in the environment. And as neither cats nor dogs are particularly popular as food in this country, disposal is an issue: 200 tonnes of dogs are destroyed each year, never mind the ones that shuffle off their canine coils naturally. So cats and dogs are a bit of an ecological nightmare. But as to whether our owning them stops us from harming the environment in other ways, we'll probably never know.

Ponds

*I*n the great green scheme of things, the eco-friendliness or otherwise of your garden pond does not have an enormous bearing on your overall environmental footprint. If you really want to bash the planet with a water feature, get a heated swimming pool (massive water and electricity use, plus harmful chlorine). But ponds get a mention because they can have a very positive impact on backyard biodiversity. Just as our gardens have become wildlife havens in a countryside that is filled with vast, chemically controlled monocultures, so ponds are important in a country where richly biodiverse wetland habitats are not what they were. Ponds provide habitat for a vast range of invertebrates, which in turn provide food that encourages birds and other garden fauna. Sure, a few gallons of murky pondwater in the corner of the garden is not going to save the planet overnight; but every pond counts.

Deep green:
Naturally 'puddled', fish-free, filled with rainwater and featuring lots of vegetation, an irregular shape with shallow edges and a bit of bog

This is the blueprint for the perfect eco-pond. If you have soil with a reasonable amount of clay, you may be able to 'puddle' (compact) the bottom of your pond-to-be with a bit of water and energetic stamping. This obviates the need for a liner, which has a bit of environmental impact (see below). Hungry fish will decrease the number and variety of interesting bugs in a pond, so leaving them out gives

201

the bugs the best chance of success. Rainwater has a low mineral content so won't encourage algal growth in the way tap water might; and lots of vegetation will oxygenate the pond and provide habitat and breeding site for teeming pond life. An irregular shape allows for more 'shoreline', also good for wildlife; and shallow edges make it easy for amphibians to crawl out and do their stuff. A boggy bit will allow for even more diversity, but this may include mosquitos and midges.

Dark green:
Wildlife-orientated pond, as above, with a butyl liner

If you don't have clay soil or want guaranteed impermeability then you will need some sort of liner; and the best-performing option is butyl rubber, which is synthesized from fossil-fuel sources. Whilst not the eco-friendliest material on the face of the planet, it is more versatile and better for pond life than alternatives such as PVC or EPDM. Using such a flexible liner makes it easy to create the natural pond shapes that give maximum wildlife benefit. Who knows whether the embodied energy or toxicity of your pond liner is offset by the lifetime eco-benefits of your pond? But it is almost always the case that any pond is better than no pond.

Quite green:
Moulded fibreglass or plastic pond

This is the 'instant' pond option, saving you the hassle of deciding what shape the pond is going to be. Materials-wise, there is probably little to choose between fibreglass, plastic and butyl: all are manufactured in energy-intensive processes and are hard to dispose of. Moulded ponds lose out to butyl only because it is not always as easy to get the shallow edges and boggy bits that give an extra wildlife boost.

Pale green:

Trendy square concrete pond full of fish, with lighting and a few fountains

It's hard to stop a pond from being 'green'. Making it out of something really energy-intensive like concrete is a start and a formal shape will reduce its potential benefits to wildlife. Adding in some fashionable underwater lighting and electric pump-powered fountains will crank up its eco-footprint a bit more. Fish will damage the biodiversity, but you can't keep a good pond down: there will always be some beneficial bugs and creatures that manage to make their home in it.

Pork, bacon and ham

(see also meat, p. 163)

As with any meat, stern environmentalists and finger-wagging veggies will tell you that there ain't no such thing as a green piggy. They do have a point. In his book Collapse, Jared Diamond notes that human settlement survived on the Pacific island of Tikopia only because the islanders took the ultimate meat sacrifice and killed all their pigs. The animals were competing with the islanders for food and anyway represented an inefficient method of food production: it took 10 kilos of their vegetables to create a kilo of pork. Modern civilization, take note. The main environmental impact of pig farming, as with all meat, is in this input:output ratio: in the case of pork, it takes 5 kilos of feed (usually cereal-based) to create one kilo of meat. As a result, vast tracts of valuable, productive land (including cleared rainforest) are given over to producing animal feed, usually with intensive methods that use fossil-fuel-derived pesticides or genetic modification. But pig farming on an intensive scale has other 'externalities', never mind all the animal-welfare indignities visited on these intelligent and sociable animals. For example, pigs produce ten times as much waste as humans, so Britain's population of nearly 5 million is not far behind us in the dungheap stakes. In the context of a small farming operation, though, pigs fit in perfectly, doing something no tractor or human can do: digging and fertilizing land whilst simultaneously turning into a magnificent edible resource.

Deep green:
'Outsourcing', preferably rare-breed

Not all of us are fortunate enough to live near a butcher who is able to offer reassurance that his pork products come from the most sustainable pigs possible. However, the raising of rare-breed pigs can be a profitable form of small-scale farming and as a result there are producers who will raise pigs to your specification so you can 'outsource' the potentially onerous task of pig-keeping. Pigs from the eight rare breeds (Gloucestershire Old Spot, Tamworth, Large Black, Berkshire, Saddleback, British Lop, Middle White, Oxford Sandy & Black) grow more slowly, are suited to the outdoor life and, crucially, taste better. Buying this way also means fewer shopping trips, as you will normally buy a whole animal and then have it butchered to your specifications for freezing or preserving in more traditional ways (air-drying, salting, brine-curing).

Dark green:
DIY

There are, of course, economies of scale in farming, which is why there are pig farms. If we all decided to raise our own pigs at home it would potentially mean a lot of feed miles and trips to the abattoir, let alone the fact that different skill levels would mean not everyone's pig-keeping was optimal for the animal or the environment. So DIY is knocked off the greenness top spot by outsourcing. However, doing it yourself gives you the ultimate reassurance that your pork has been produced to exacting welfare and environmental specifications. The DIY option only works for those of us with truly massive gardens or a bit of land and is only a good choice environmentally if the pigs are integrated into your own domestic ecosystem: eating waste food like orchard windfalls and having all their wastes used on your land. Like all livestock, pigs are most sustainable when they form part of a mixed, closed-loop farm in which all the resources are re-used and recycled.

Quite green:
Preferably rare-breed, bought direct or from a farmers' market or good butcher

A growing number of small producers sell by mail order and on the Internet as well as direct from the farm, bringing tasty, traditional, outdoor-reared pork products within reach of everyone. And if you really want to check whether your pigs are as eco-friendly as possible, you can always visit the farms, too. Pork products from farmers' markets or really good butchers are more likely to have been sustain-ably reared: both of these outlets offer you the chance, lacking in supermarkets, to quiz the producer or retailer directly about how the meat was raised.

Light green:
Organic pork products

It is perfectly possible for pork to be produced to an incredibly high standard yet not be organic. The organic certification process is too onerous and expensive for some producers and ensuring your pigs have a certified organic diet on certified organic land can be a costly business. Hence many of the smaller producers sell pork that doesn't have the 'badge' but meets or exceeds organic standards. If you are not buying direct or from a producer or butcher you can look in the eye, then the Soil Association's organic standard is the best guarantee that your pork and bacon has been produced in the most sustainable way. And it also means that all the animals' feed is GM-free, removing another potential environmental issue. There is no formal 'free-range' label for pigs as there is for, say, hens, so free-range pork may just mean pigs that had a brief spell outdoors before spending most of their lives in crowded indoor conditions.

Not even a little bit green:
Any old pork and bacon, preferably from overseas, probably processed

Over 70 per cent of pigs in Britain are raised indoors in intensive systems. With big inputs – of high-protein, cereal-based feed and all the power and infrastructure needed to run large facilities – and major outputs of slurry, these represent the unsustainable end of pig production. However, British welfare standards for pigs are higher than elsewhere in the world: for example, we no longer allow sows to be confined in stalls all their lives. So imported pork is likely to have been produced even more intensively and it will, of course, have an added food-miles issue. Overseas pork that has been processed in Britain, say into bacon or ham, can be badged as British. And low-grade processed pork products will have been mucked about with to compensate for their poor quality, with water and artificial flavourings added in industrial processes that increase their sorry load on the environment yet further.

MORE INFORMATION
'Outsourced' pigs: www.numberonepig.co.uk
Rare-breed pork: info via www.rbst.org.uk
List of farmers' markets: www.farmersmarkets.net

Potatoes

We like our spuds, to the tune of 100 kilos each per year – and the 6 million tonnes we produce in Britain just about matches our communal potato habit. (We're no match for Poland, though, with almost half the population and twice the potato tonnage.) There has been huge concentration in UK potato production in the last fifty years, with only 3,000 registered growers today (compared to 77,000 in 1960) and a doubling in the yield per hectare. Potatoes affect the environment through the energy needed to grow them, much of which goes into manufacturing the various fungicides, herbicides and insecticides they require. (The government approved the UK trial in 2007 of GM potatoes that have been engineered to resist late blight and thus to need radically fewer applications of fungicide.) Then there's storage: anything that isn't a 'new' potato (see below) is likely to have spent some time in storage, which may mean refrigeration and more chemicals. However, nearly half of the energy use in a potato's 'life cycle' is in transport and preparation because, obviously, it's a heavy crop that often needs lengthy cooking.

Deep green:
Your own potatoes

This knocks out the food miles straight away (apart from getting the seed potatoes from the garden centre). Potato cultivation, incidentally, is the only way in which you could ever hope to be self-sufficient from a back garden because it is the only temperate-climate staple crop that gives big yields in small spaces. Grow spuds in towers (of old tyres, say, for maximum recycling effect) and you can make best use of the vertical space in your garden. It's also possible to store potatoes in a completely zero-energy way by 'clamping' them in a closed mound of earth, so you could potentially eat your own harvest through the autumn, winter and early spring. However, climate change may make things too warm for clamping – which relies on cool conditions – to be practical for much longer.

Dark green:
Organic new potatoes from Britain, in season

The new-potato season starts in April and runs through to July, with Jersey Royals traditionally the first 'local' new-season spud to make it to market. New potatoes get placed high in the green rankings because they need less storage energy than 'maincrop' varieties, which are lifted in the late summer/early autumn and stored through the winter. There are no conclusive data on whether organic potatoes are more energy-efficient. Organic potato cultivation offers only about 60 per cent of the yield that can be achieved with artificial fertilizers and chemical treatments, so it needs more land to get the same result. It also needs more fuel-guzzling machinery (mechanical weeders, for example). However, conventional cultivation does use very heavy loads of pesticides (mainly fungicides to ward off blight): at 13 kilos per hectare, it is three times the quantity used on cereal crops. There has been a strong upward trend in pesticide usage since the late 1990s and in a recent survey 32 per cent of potato samples were found to have residues. Whilst the residues themselves are not thought to be a health issue, the unnecessary presence in the environment of substances, some of which are carcinogenic, toxic and endocrine-disrupting, cannot be a good thing from an environmental point of view. Large quantities of sulphuric acid are also applied to conventionally grown potatoes to kill off the haulms (plants) before harvesting.

Quite green:
Organic British maincrop potatoes

Maincrop potatoes are, in essence, anything that isn't classified as a 'new' potato. Their skins are left to 'set' before they are harvested; thereafter, they can be stored for up to ten months at a temperature of around 4°C. This long storage quality is what has made potatoes such a valuable year-round staple crop; it is also why we have only a relatively small need for imports. However, storing potatoes, which are at risk from all sorts of pests and diseases, is a tricky business. It can be done without refrigeration, but this becomes necessary for longer-term storage. And in some cases post-harvest chemicals are used to prevent the potatoes from sprouting and catching fungal infections whilst the crop lurks in the store. So maincrop potatoes are likely to have a higher 'energy burden' than new potatoes; and non-organic ones may have been treated with post-harvest chemicals as well as all the chemicals they cop in the growing season. Organic potatoes are not grown entirely without chemical intervention, though: copper-based fungicides are permitted and are essential when there is a risk of blight infecting the crop. Maincrop potatoes are available all year round but harvested in September and October.

Pale green:
Any old potatoes from the supermarket

Unless you go looking for interesting varieties or buy from farmers' markets or other small-scale outlets, the chances are that the potatoes you are buying have been grown on a fairly industrial scale with many chemical inputs. None of this is necessarily a health issue; however, conventional production is not helpful for biodiversity, which has declined sharply since the advent of industrial farming. One could also argue that, in general, conventionally grown maincrop potatoes are a pretty inefficient staple crop in environmental terms, since their cultivation and storage requires so much in the way of energy and chemicals. Dried pasta is probably a greener choice as a winter staple – but you can't make chips with it . . .

Not even a little bit green:
Chips

All the energy of potato-growing, plus vast amounts of energy-intensive vegetable oil (or even animal fat) plus loads of heat for cooking. And if you buy them from a fast-food outlet or dodgy chippy, chances are they'll be made of the most industrially produced spuds available. The sad truth for hungry eco-warriors is that chips aren't green. But sometimes even the hardest greenies have to let their hair down . . . (see also bacon, aeroplanes, etc.).

Potato season

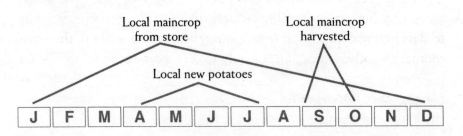

212

Rice

When it comes to staple crops, rice is the big one, providing more calories to humans than any other single food. Its environmental footprint is pretty chunky, too, thanks to a global cultivated area six times the size of the UK. After the burning of fossil fuels and the flatulence of livestock, rice-growing is the third biggest human-generated source of methane, a potent greenhouse gas. And since the 'green revolution', in which high-yield Western agricultural technologies were exported to developing countries in the second half of the twentieth century, rice production has also involved plenty of artificial fertilizers and pesticides; and a great deal more water than it once needed. Given the immense scale of the world market for rice, biotechnology companies are keen to promote genetically modified (GM) strains too.

Deep green:
Local staple foods

Why eat an Asian staple if you live in Britain? We're doing just fine with wheat, oats and barley, thank you very much, is what the true UK deep greenie would say if offered a supply of rice. One could argue that buying sustainably farmed rice provides essential support to developing countries, thus stopping them laying waste to the environment in other ways; but it surely makes more sense to do this via high-value imports for which there is no local substitute, such as coffee, tea or chocolate.

RICE

Dark green:
Organic risotto rice

The debate about the relative merits of organic vs high-tech rice production is far from over (see organic brown rice, below). But given that high yields are claimed to be possible without energy-intensive inputs of artificial fertility and pest control, it gets a green ranking. Short-grain risotto rice is grown mainly in Italy, so arguably it's a more local product for the British. But in reality, with trucking ten times more polluting per tonne/kilometre than shipping, there's probably little to choose between the eco-footprint of Italian risotto rice and, say, Thai long-grain.

Quite green:
Organic brown rice

The staple food of the hair-shirt hippy gets knocked into third place for reasons discussed above. Like wholemeal flour, brown rice under-goes less processing so its production uses marginally less energy; and importantly, it retains nutrients that may have to be added back to white rice. As to the organic debate, it goes something like this: the 'green revolution' (using 'modern' agricultural techniques) enabled greater yields to be obtained, thus saving millions of hectares from the plough. A widespread move to lower-yielding organic production would ultimately mean more deforestation and thus less biodiversity. And if the costs and impacts of pesticides and herbicides are a problem (which they are: 50,000 Chinese farmers are poisoned each year), GM technology will save the day – experimental strains with built-in insecticides have been developed, for example. On the other side of the fence, organic proponents say that you can in fact get higher yields with growing techniques such as polyculture (e.g. raising fish or ducks in the paddies as well), sequential planting (with other crops such as wheat or barley) or planting multiple cultivars rather than monocultures. Just to complicate matters further, brown rice does of course take twice as much cooking time, which could tip the ecological balance in favour of white rice . . . (but maybe not if the white rice is parboiled or 'easy cook', in which case its primary production will have used more energy). Phew.

Not particularly green:
American long-grain rice

Whilst much non-organic rice cultivation all over the world uses energy-intensive and potentially polluting agrochemical inputs, conventional rice production in the USA is highly mechanized and therefore even more of a fossil-fuel guzzler. And whilst GM rice is banned in this country, anyone with concerns over this technology should note that traces of a herbicide-tolerant GM variety have turned up in American long-grain rice sold in the UK. This was not considered a health risk but it does illustrate the difficulty of containing such crops in the environment.

Salads and lettuce

*T*he bagged salad has joined the battery hen and the air-freighted green bean as one of the icons of food unsustainability. This is largely on account of its resource-intensive, often long-distance genesis. Much salad eaten in the UK, particularly in the cooler months, comes from southern Spain, where it gets heavy doses of fertilizers and pesticides, a wash in chlorine solution shortly after picking, then a 900-mile refrigerated lorry journey in controlled-atmosphere packaging before it reaches our supermarket shelves. This represents a lot of fuel and resources for a few leaves. Boosters of the bagged salad suggest that they have brought more salad variety into our lives and stimulated the consumption of green things; the British Nutrition Foundation points out that bagged salad is better than no salad at all. We are eating more, for sure: our salad consumption rose 18 per cent between 1992 and 2002. But the value of the salad market grew 90 per cent in the same period, so someone is making good money out of our healthy habit. The big question is whether the environmental cost of salad outweighs its value to human consumers.

Deep green:
Grow your own

Home growing is often the choice of the deep greenie, but it's not always easy. In the case of salads and lettuce, it's not too much effort to be deep green. Salad crops are easy to grow; some, such as wild rocket and sorrel, are perennial so will keep coming back every year for little or no effort on your part. Home growing means that the all-important plot-to-plate journey is minimized, which also means your own salads are likely to have much higher levels of nutrients than leaves that have been lurking in a cold lorry or storeroom for days. Choosing a range of varieties means you can extend the season, say with lamb's lettuce or winter purslane for the cooler months. And a greenhouse offers the possibility of year-round home-grown salad.

Dark green:
Seasonal, local, organic, outdoor salads

The outdoor salad season in Britain runs from around May to October, so salad with few food miles should be readily available at farmers' markets, local greengrocers and supermarkets. Whilst the use of pesticides on salads in the UK has declined in recent years, conventionally grown outdoor crops still get, on average, two doses each of insecticides, herbicides and fungicides during their short growing season. In the most recent study, 30 per cent of lettuces sampled contained pesticide residues; however, this is an improvement on previous years. Some conventional growers use a balance of traditional and high-tech strategies to reduce the chemical load on the plants, for example crop rotations and physical protection against predators. This can, however, mean acreages of protective mesh covering the countryside, which leaves the environmentally minded salad-eater to contemplate whether a brief pass with an insecticide is better, in sustainability terms, than large areas of crop protection, whose production, application and disposal all carry an environmental cost too. Unlike protected, indoor crops, which are susceptible to mildew, outdoor salads are easy to produce in organic systems; and as well as having had minimal spraying will also not have been chlorine-washed.

Quite green:
Just seasonal and local

What if you want an organic lettuce in February? Chances are you won't be able to find a British one, so you'll need to look overseas. At which point a debate over the relative merits of imported organics versus local hot-house varieties arises. Although the study hasn't been done for lettuce, for other produce there is often little to choose between the two options in energy terms, because the food miles of something grown where it is warm can be balanced out by the artificial heating its cultivation will need where it is cool. So neither option is particularly good: winter abstinence and sticking to seasonal, local produce (organic or not) makes for the most eco-friendly salad behaviour. Anyway, what use is a 130-calories-per-kilo lettuce on a cold winter's day?

Not even a little bit green:
Imported salads during the British season

It is questionable whether a 900-mile refrigerated truck journey can ever be justifiable for a perishable, low-calorie crop like lettuce and salads. But during our own growing season it seems well beyond the eco pale to go looking for imported salad. Seekers after the least green salad option might also look out for Californian lettuce, on account of its long, air-freighted food miles.

Salad season

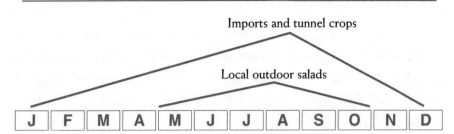

Imports and tunnel crops

Local outdoor salads

| J | F | M | A | M | J | J | A | S | O | N | D |

Salmon

As well as being high on the list of ultra-healthy gourmet delicacies, salmon also tops the list of foods with serious environmental issues. According to the Marine Conservation Society, stocks of wild North Atlantic salmon have halved in the last twenty years; the reasons cited for the population decline are many and complex and include overfishing, environmental change, pollution, habitat reduction and aquaculture. Despite this, UK salmon consumption has risen rapidly in recent years, tripling between 1992 and 2000. Almost all of this growing salmon habit is catered for by farmed salmon, whose environmental charge sheet is about as long as it gets.

Deep green:
Wild salmon from a sustainable fishery

Taking a sustainable quantity of a wild food is always the very greenest choice, because nature takes care of all the feeding and husbandry, which otherwise create potentially huge environmental impacts. It's also the best gastronomic choice, as anyone who has tasted wild salmon alongside even the best farmed stuff will know. However, finding a sustainable fishery is not easy these days, with so many sources of Atlantic salmon considered depleted. Unless you are fortunate enough to know local salmon anglers who are sure of their stocks, the best option is to look to the Pacific and to Alaskan wild salmon, which is widely stocked in supermarkets. Fish farming is banned in Alaska (because of concerns over its impact on the wild stock) and the Marine Stewardship Council has certified the wild salmon fishery there as sustainable. It may travel a long way to our shelves, but the journey will have been by sea, the least fuel-intensive way of transporting food.

Not even a little bit green:
Farmed salmon

Salmon farming is big business in the UK, principally in Scotland where it accounts for 40 per cent of all food exports by value. Campaigners argue that this comes at a serious cost and that salmon farming is one of the most environmentally destructive forms of agriculture there is. For a start, there is no getting away from the 'feed conversion' problem. Salmon are carnivorous fish and it takes 3–5 kilos of wild fish to create one kilo of farmed. No advanced mathematical skills are necessary to see that this is not a sustainable state of affairs, particularly when the majority of the world's wild fish stocks are in decline. The pollution caused by salmon farms ranges from concentrated effluent and waste feed, which affects the local aquatic environment, to concentrations of sea lice which a US study has confirmed have a serious impact on wild fish, to releases of pesticides and antibiotics. Then there are 'escapes': hundreds of thousands of farmed salmon get out of their pens every year and interbreed with the wild population, potentially reducing its ability to survive. Organic farmed salmon is available, certified (controversially) by the Soil Association. Fish farmed this way eat the offcuts of caught wild fish and therefore have an arguably more sustainable diet; although only by 2010 will all their feed come from MSC-certified sustainable fisheries. They are stocked at lower densities than conventionally farmed salmon but this is still up to 30,000 per cage for a fish that naturally prefers to spend its life migrating huge distances from fresh water to the sea and back. And drugs and chemicals to treat disease and infestations are still allowed. It is difficult to see how even the most eco-friendly salmon farming could ever register on the green scale.

Shoes

Will careful shoe-sourcing stop climate change? Probably not. Of all the things we wear, shoes have the potential to have the lowest eco-footprint for the simple reason that they can last for years, diluting the impact of their manufacture. There is much more concern over the use of sweatshop labour and animal products in the shoe industry than whether our footwear choices are belching CO_2 or laying waste to ecosystems. Still, look at things from a purely environmental perspective and a sliding scale of shoes emerges.

Deep green:
Hemp shoes with recycled-car-tyre soles

It is surely impossible to get more squeakily green than this in the world of footwear. Hemp (see also clothing, p. 68) gets huge eco-points for being a low-impact crop that grows locally. The resultant material is tough and has many of the qualities to which higher-tech materials aspire: breathability and natural antibacterial properties. With discarded vehicle tyres presenting a tricky waste problem, putting them to good use as shoe soles (which happens by necessity in many developing countries) beats landfill or incineration any day.

Dark green:
Hand-made local leather shoes

A sharp intake of breath from vegans and vegetarians is to be expected at the presence of leather so high up the rankings. And it is a controversial placing, for leather requires animal husbandry, which is responsible for major environmental impacts; and the tanning process can create high levels of pollution. However, as long as we live in a world in which people consume dairy products or meat, there will also be a renewable source of top-quality shoemaking material of which we might as well take advantage. Leather's immense durability means that as long as you are selective and sparing in your shoe purchases and take old-fashioned good care of your shoes, their overall environmental impact will be minimized over time.

Quite green:
Vegan and vegetarian shoes

For the many people who reject leather on ideological grounds, there is a growing range of footwear options beyond hemp and car tyres. Man-made materials such as Lorica and Vegetan, which uses a combination of cotton and polyurethane, are breathable, durable and avoid the worrying aesthetic of less sophisticated plastic shoes. Looked at from a severely environmental point of view, though, it should not be forgotten than such materials are derived largely from fossil fuels and cotton (see also p. 70), which is hardly an ecologically angelic substance either.

Not particularly green:
PVC thigh boots

They may have a certain irresistible charm to many, but the sort of footwear that might grace a particularly serious night out is not ideal for the environmentally minded. PVC (see also p. 133) is a material whose manufacture and lifespan can result in noxious emissions; thigh boots obviously maximize the quantity of it.

Not even a little bit green:
Imelda Marcos-esque shoe habit

If shiny boots are your only shoes, though, they won't have anything like the same impact as a major shoe habit. A large collection, even of vegan shoes, will soon crank up your footwear's footprint to impressive levels.

Showers

As many items in this book show, you don't have to wear a hair shirt to be green. Dishwashers, for example (see p. 272), are greener than almost all forms of washing up by hand. Hurrah! Achieving serious greenness in the world of showering does, however, mean reaching for the scratchy garment. Yes, they may use less water overall than having a bath: on average, 35 litres per five-minute shower compared with the 80 litres devoured by the standard bath. But showering comfort is all about warmth and flow: and the simple fact is that the tropical thunderstorm feel of a good modern power shower (which can kick out 20+ litres per minute) beats the feeble trickle of a miserly old-school shower any day. We are buying more powerful showers and using them more often, so the ecological footprint of an act once considered environmentally virtuous is on the up. Although showers account on average for only 5 of the 20 per cent of domestic water used by bathing, their contribution is rising.

Deep green:

Short, infrequent, rainwater showers, heated by solar power in the summer and biofuels in the winter — 'camping' option

This involves a ten-quid (or home-made) solar bag shower that you fill from a water butt, leave in the sun, then hang from a tree for a brief sun-warmed drenching. In winter, rainwater heated by a wood fire then delivered by a similar gravity-fed contraption would do the trick. All completely carbon- and water-neutral. But with numerous disadvantages involving varying degrees of physical and social discomfort and inconvenience, this is strictly for the ideologically committed.

Dark green:
Short, infrequent, rainwater showers, heated by solar power in the summer and biofuels in the winter – 'household' option

Given the technology involved, this is strictly for the financially committed (or for super-confident DIY all-rounders). You will need a rain-harvesting system (see p. 277) to store and pipe the rainwater to your shower, plus a solar hot-water system (see p. 139) to heat the water in summer. (This will also mean not having a combi boiler, which is incompatible with solar hot water.) And although solar hot water does make a contribution all year round, you will need a biofuel heating system (see p. 139) to heat the water in winter. All of this is possible and it will also take care of all your space- and water-heating needs. But it comes at a price – probably approaching £10,000. Your reward, however, will be an environmentally friendly shower that doesn't involve naked shivering in the garden. It's also worth pointing out that any of the three parts of this 'dark green' suggestion will make a dent in your shower's ecological footprint.

Quite green:
Short, infrequent, gas-heated showers using mains-pressure water and with a water-saving showerhead or flow regulator

Sticking with the short and infrequent is clearly a key way towards showering virtue. The less you primp and preen, the more the planet heaves a sigh of relief. Gas heating wins over electricity because, although electric showers tend to have a lower flow (of as little as 3.5 litres per minute, which also makes them a bit rubbish), electric water-heating ultimately produces more CO_2, for reasons explained below. Mains pressure (rather than gravity-fed water from a tank) delivers a decent pressure of one bar or more: this means a water-saving showerhead or flow regulator will work effectively, giving you what feels like a decent shower for about 6 litres per minute of flow.

Pale green:
Short, infrequent visits to a weedy electric shower

Even the feeblest electric showers use over 7kW of electricity to get the water from the 10°C mains temperature up to the 40°C at which we like to shower. Over a year, a disappointing five-minute daily session in one of these will still knock over 80kg of CO_2 into the atmosphere. Plus you'll probably want to prolong the shower to compensate for the weedy flow, thus using as much as if not more water than average and cranking up the power use and emissions.

Not even a little bit green:
Long, frequent, luxurious visits to a multi-jet power shower

This is the express route to massive water use. A high-end multi-jet power shower can blast out 38 litres per minute, meaning that your five-minute shower now uses twice as much as the average bath. Allow for two such luxurious experiences a day for each member of a four-person family, and showering alone is now accounting for ten times the UK national average daily water use. Even so, this could be dark green if you had the rain-harvesting/solar/biofuel option and a vast storage tank; but to get the 550,000 litres your annual showering now demands, you will also need to live somewhere seriously rainy – say Borrowdale in the Lake District – and have a truly enormous roof area of around 300 square metres to collect it all.

Soap and detergents

*I*s it possible to be clean and green? It depends on your definition of clean. If cleanliness is acquired through lots of deep, hot baths, over-packaged synthetic soaps and shampoos, and clothes that have acquired that 'meadow-fresh' scent without the involvement of any meadows, then it comes at a high environmental cost. If, however, you have a much more relaxed definition of what it means to be clean, then the planet will thank you for it. The biggest eco-impacts of washing ourselves and our clothes come through the use and heating of water (see baths, showers, washing clothes, pp. 27, 226 and 267). But our choice of cleaning products does make a difference too, in their production, packaging and final passage out into the environment.

Deep green:
Standards of personal hygiene from a bygone era

Before the soap industry got us all warily sniffing our armpits to assess whether we had 'BO' or some such invented condition, we all got along fine in a world that probably smelled a great deal riper than it does today. As far as soap and detergents are concerned, all it takes to save the planet is an attitude shift. Radically reduced washing, bathing and clothes-washing will make a big dent in your eco-footprint, mainly through reduced water and fuel use. And if, on the rare occasions that washing happens, you use natural products such as home-made soap made from vegetable oil and processed wood ash, your footprint will be reduced further still. The only problem with this approach, of course, is that everybody in the household – and preferably the local community – needs to adopt it in order for everyone to be happy with it.

Dark green:
Hippy soaps and detergents, used sparingly

There is a lot of funny stuff in the things with which we keep ourselves and our clothes clean. The ingredient 'parfum', for example, can cover a range of synthetic fragrance ingredients, some of which have a tendency to 'bio-accumulate' in our bodies. Preservative parabens are oestrogen mimics and endocrine disrupters. Sodiums lauryl and laureth sulphate can cause skin irritation; antibacterial ingredients can kill the good bugs too, helping to create over-clean environments. Many soaps also contain animal fats, a traditional soap ingredient and useful by-product of the meat industry. Arguably, making soap is a good way of using unwanted animal fats that would otherwise need to be disposed of; but it's not a concept that is to everyone's taste. As for detergents, the phosphates they contain to soften the water account for around 15 per cent of all phosphates entering watercourses, where they stimulate algal growth that depletes the aquatic environment. The detergent industry suggests that removing the phosphates at the sewage-treatment stage, rather than taking them out of detergents, is the best solution: but nitrogen and phosphate removal is an energy-intensive part of the sewage-treatment process. To get away from these myriad complex environmental issues, using soaps and detergents based on natural, plant-derived ingredients or with no phosphates will make your 'greywater' as pleasant as possible.

Not even a little bit green:

Every conceivable personal and laundry cleaning product available, used with obsessive frequency

See that person over there with the brilliant white yet ultra-soft clothes, hair that has both volume and poise and hands so clean that he could perform open-heart surgery without gloves? Total eco-criminal. Such cleanliness is most definitely not next to environmental godliness. Lots and lots of washing means high energy and water use, and loads of lovely detergent-laden greywater for the overloaded sewage system to deal with. Being ultra clean probably involves the full gamut of those entirely unnecessary cleaning products that are pure inventions of rabid sales departments: facial wipes, fabric conditioners, hair conditioners, liquid antibacterial soap from a complex plastic dispenser (ideal for hospitals, but for the home?). All of this stuff drives industrial activity that could be much more productively redirected, and creates unnecessary pollution and mountains of waste. Dirty is the new clean.

Strawberries

*I*t's a shame that something so fragrant, delicate and delicious is so beset by environmental issues. But it's the strawberry's very popularity that has made it such a bête noire of environmentalists. First, there's the issue of extending the season: strawberries fruit naturally outdoors in Britain for a mere two months before we have to put away the cream and sugar for another year. Sensing that there are many who would prefer a longer dalliance with this fine fruit, British growers have now extended the season to nine months, with heated glasshouse and also polytunnel cultivation meaning that we need forgo patriotic strawberries only from January to March. The resultant expanding acreage of polytunnels has caused local outcries. Then there are agrochemicals: strawberries need 30 per cent fewer if grown indoors, but their susceptibility to soil-borne disease means the soil may have been sterilized with methyl bromide, a class-one ozone depleter that will be banned in 2008. Finally, imported strawberries carry heavy eco-baggage too, what with excessive air miles and wetland depletion being two charges laid at their door. Given these and the many other issues involved, it is not easy to discern shades of green for strawberries with accuracy. Here's a stab.

Deep green:
Grow your own, go without for most of the year

We managed without the year-round strawberry until a few years ago; is life with nine strawberry-free months really so bad? It's a matter of opinion, clearly. But on the difficulty and skill scale, backyard strawberry-growing is not too tricky and even if you don't have a garden, container growing works fine. What you will notice is a marked difference in eating quality. Most commercial strawberries are of a single variety, Elsanta, whose tough skin can put up with the travelling that supermarket distribution entails. The more delicate and perishable varieties you can grow yourself are a taste sensation compared to these; and such intensity of flavour is often linked to nutritional value, for which strawberries are famed. For the other nine months of the year, strawberry jam or ice cream can provide a constant reminder of the fleeting summer flavour to come.

Dark green:

'Pick-your-own' outdoor strawberries, self-denial for the other nine months

This means you will eat strawberries only in their natural season and – assuming you haven't chartered a private jet to get to the farm – the effect of food miles will be minimized. It is highly unlikely that you will find organic outdoor strawberries, though, because field cultivation makes it harder to control the botrytis and mould to which the fruit is particularly susceptible.

Quite green:

British organic strawberries in season

Only a tiny percentage of the British strawberry crop is organic, but it does make it into the supermarkets in season. In conventional cultivation, strawberries do get heavy doses of pesticides and about 70 per cent contain residues, so choosing organic largely gets round this issue and all of the energy needed to create the agrochemicals. Soil sterilants won't have been used in organic cultivation and the strawberries will have been grown in real soil rather than peat or an artificial substrate. However, they will have been grown under cover, which is debated below.

Pale green:
British strawberries from August to November

The vast majority of these will have been grown in polytunnels. Why does this get a green ranking (albeit a marginal one)? It's a tricky call. Here's what both sides have to say. The pro-tunnel-growing lobby claims the following: botrytis and mildew can be almost eliminated, because tunnels can be kept dry; as a result the pesticide load is 30 per cent lower than in outdoor systems. Around 80–90 per cent of the crop is 'saleable', compared to 50–70 per cent from open-air cultivation. Polytunnels reduce the need for imports. The tunnels are covered only during the production months and look no worse than the plastic mulch or fleece that is increasingly used in agriculture; and the plastic can be recycled. The anti-tunnel lobby's claims are as follows: vast amounts of largely fossil-fuel-derived materials are needed to build the tunnels: up to 2 hectares of plastic and 7.5 kilometres of steel tubing per hectare of growing. The plastic is not recycled to any significant degree. There are negative impacts on local wildlife (from soil micro-organisms to birds). And localized flooding is caused by the tunnels whilst at the same time, and somewhat ironically, artificial irrigation is also needed. And, of course, a sea of tunnels is a blot on the landscape. The inescapable fact is that if you want a guaranteed supply of strawberries outside our natural outdoor growing season, then it's a choice between imports (food miles and possibly lower growing standards) and polytunnels (see above for all the issues). Which you think is the best choice may depend on whether or not you live near to a sea of polytunnels, but in energy terms, unheated, local, protected growing beats imports, whether they come in by lorry or air.

Not particularly green:
British strawberries in April, May and December

If you want strawberries during these months, then some heat is involved, which means energy. Despite the increasing efficiency of glasshouse production – for example using combined heat and power systems to generate electricity as well as heat, or venting CO_2 into the greenhouse rather than the atmosphere to encourage the crop – it has been shown to be little better (if at all) in energy terms than road-freighted imports that have been grown without heat. It's a lot better than air-freighted produce, though.

Not particularly green either:
Imported strawberries during our own season

They won't taste any better. Why bother?

Not even a little bit green:
Any strawberries from January to March

The depths of winter provide the only break in Britain's expanded strawberry season, so it's imports only in these months. You can get hold of organic produce, but the growing standards overseas may not be as high and the ecological cost of all the food miles for what is an entirely unnecessary food purchase must surely cancel out any organic benefits in this case. Never mind their road miles, the irrigation demands of strawberries grown in Spain are said to be responsible for a 50 per cent reduction in water flowing to wetlands in a national park. Strawberries from further afield than Europe are likely to be air-freighted, which cranks up the CO_2 per punnet to as much as the equivalent of eleven average school runs in a car.

Strawberry season

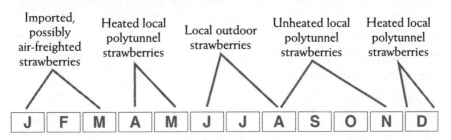

Imported, possibly air-freighted strawberries

Heated local polytunnel strawberries

Local outdoor strawberries

Unheated local polytunnel strawberries

Heated local polytunnel strawberries

| J | F | M | A | M | J | J | A | S | O | N | D |

Sugar

We eat, on average, 35 kilos of sugar each per year, three-quarters of it in sweet foods and soft drinks. Sugar accounts for 2 per cent of the food transported by road in the UK and 17 per cent of all our food imports. Its production and refining, whether from sugar cane or beet, have all sorts of environmental issues. But what differentiates sugar from other foods is that it we don't need it, physiologically: all it does is provide calories with no other nutritional benefits. We can get by quite happily on the natural sugars in the foods we eat: the entire teeth-rotting, fuel-guzzling, topsoil-stripping, pesticide-intensive business of growing and refining sugar is entirely unnecessary. Which makes it a bit tricky from a strictly environmental point of view.

Deep green:
Honey

Clearly, those on the hessian-wearing wing of the deep green tendency would happily do without any artificial sweeteners as part of their overall planet-saving strategy. They would, however, do better to lighten up and choose honey, which beats sugar hands down as a sweetener on ecological grounds. Apiculture makes a net contribution to the environment, because bees provide essential pollination services for many plants and crops: it is said that every third mouthful of food we eat depends on them. Honey also has antibacterial and antimicrobial qualities and its pollen content is valued by hayfever sufferers. Altogether a greener way to sweeten things if you have decided to ditch the hessian.

Dark green:
Organic or Fairtrade unrefined dark sugar

Organic sugar is almost certain to be from sugar cane. Farming sugar beet organically is difficult because the crop competes poorly with weeds, which are kept down in conventional farming with generous doses of herbicide. British Sugar, the sole UK processor of sugar beet, stopped producing organic sugar in 2004, citing lack of demand. So sustainably farmed sugar will come from the tropics, where organic cultivation mitigates the impact that sugar monocultures have on the environment, such as declining biodiversity and fertilizer runoff. Choosing Fairtrade means that poorly paid tropical producers, who do not enjoy the generous subsidies paid to European beet sugar producers, will at least get a guaranteed price for their crop. And unrefined sugar will not have gone through purifying and decolourizing processes which require more energy and resources. There is also a chance that its natural molasses content will mean that unrefined sugar contains a bit of goodness along with its sweetness.

Pale green:
Beet sugar

Which in Britain means Silver Spoon, the brand name under which locally produced beet sugar is sold. On the one hand, beet sugar, which accounts for 60 per cent of the sugar we eat, is not particularly friendly to the environment. It gets the largest herbicide dose of any crop; and the resultant weed-free fields are not great places for biodiversity. And beet harvesting removes hundreds of thousands of tonnes of topsoil from the fields. On the other hand, sugar beet fits into crop rotations, thus making better use of land than a monoculture crop. If it is spring-sown, the fields provide both nesting sites and food for some bird species. The stripped topsoil is sold on and re-used and the by-products of both growing and processing can be sold as animal feed and fertilizer. And the food miles are fewer than for tropical sugar. However, your view of beet sugar may also be tainted by the fact that in buying British beet sugar you are subsidizing producers who are already heavily subsidized, whereas Fairtrade sugar is arguably delivering the money to someone who really needs it.

Not even a little bit green:
White refined cane sugar

This is the least environmentally friendly option for a food that is not, in essence, particularly environmentally friendly. The monoculture growing of sugar cane results in soil losses that are a hundred times higher than they would naturally be. The crop needs irrigation and plenty of fertilizer and this results in agricultural runoffs, some of which are said to be responsible for damaging Australia's Great Barrier Reef. Cane sugar has made a longer journey than beet; and its refinement to produce the stable, pure-white (and entirely nutrient-free) substance we have come to expect involves energy-intensive industrial processes.

Tea

The first analysis looking at the environmental cost of tea was arguably undertaken by William Cobbett in the early nineteenth century. Incensed by the effort needed to create what he considered to be a nutritionally worthless beverage, Cobbett calculated that the cost to an honest working family of a daily tea habit – and all the fire-making and labour that it entailed in 1820 – was almost double that of brewing your own wholesome beer. Today, the 60 billion cups of tea we drink each year may be easier to make, but their brewing still guzzles 2.8TWh of energy, which would keep a small power station busy and could surely be turned to more constructive purposes. Then there are the packaging, shipping and pesticide-intensive monocultures in which most tea is grown in the first place. All in all, our nice cup of tea takes a chunk out of the biosphere. But would the biosphere be worth living in without it?

Deep green:
Make your own hippy tea, brew it cold or with biofuels

It's not always the case that the deepest green option is the least fun (in fact with coffee it's the opposite, see p. 75). But it is with tea. Stern greenies will side with Cobbett, frowning at a product that is somewhat addictive and completely unnecessary. However, such ascetics might disagree with him about the value of homebrew as a replacement and instead drink their own herbal tea, a vast, free supply of which is all around us and needs no destructive agriculture, fuel-burning shipping or resource-intensive packaging. Dandelion, nettle, mint and many others have their own gustatory and medicinal qualities, even if they lack the caffeine lift that tea provides. Serious hair-shirters could opt for a long, slow infusion in cold water to save even more energy; others looking for a hippy cuppa that is both carbon-neutral and hot will boil up the water on a wood-burning stove or equivalent.

Dark green:
Fairtrade organic tea, loose

There's no getting round the food miles issue with *Camellia sinensis*, which only grows in places distant from the UK. But even the monster British tea habit equates to less than 200,000 tonnes per year, which is only one tenth of the capacity of a single large container ship. Hardly a heavyweight commodity; and it does of course have a great deal of value in trade terms, particularly for developing countries. However, this value doesn't always translate into much for tea workers, so look for the Fairtrade logo that means that certain standards of welfare and environmental protection will have been adhered to. Unlike coffee (see p. 75), tea tends to be grown in large, monocultural plantations with all the usual negative impacts of such agriculture on biodiversity and soil quality. Regular doses of hazardous agrochemicals are also used in such systems, residues of which have recently been detected in tea, albeit below 'safe' levels. Organic tea cultivation, whilst lower yielding, is better for the local ecosystems. Biodynamic teas, which take the organic concept even further (see p. 283), are also available. Buying tea loose rather than in bags means you can be more frugal with your tea dosage; and it removes another manufacturing and packaging step.

Not particularly green:
Ludicrously over-packaged teabags

Tea aficionados shun teabags, principally on the grounds that they often use the inferior 'fannings' and 'dust' left over from tea processing. Lack of any organic certification will mean that the tea may have been grown in a rather cavalier manner; but to boost your cuppa's eco-footprint, choose ultra-packaged varieties, where the teabag is contained within another bag, which itself is in a cardboard box that is then wrapped in plastic.

Not even a little bit green:
Decaffeinated tea

It may be harsh to suggest that those wanting tea without the caffeine should seek another beverage, but it makes environmental sense. The stimulant is removed either with carbon dioxide gas under heat and pressure or with solvents: both of these are resource-intensive industrial processes that are entirely unnecessary. And the solvent method is said to remove the antioxidant goodness for which tea is famed. So if you ever ponder a cup of decaff tea with skimmed milk (another product from which the very essence is sucked, at extra effort, for no good reason; see p. 176), visualize that iconic polar bear teetering on melting ice and have a nice cup of nettle instead.

Telephones

*E*ven telephones have green nuances, although some of them are rather fine. The traditional telephone network, with its thousands of kilometres of cable, fleets of vans and trucks, exchanges, buildings and infrastructure, does have a significant environmental cost. Mobile networks' footprint includes base stations and their masts, which themselves have raised concerns about radiation. And, of course, fancy modern handsets, whether related to a mobile network or a house-bound digital cordless base station, all need charging.

Deep green:
Old-school fixed-wire phone

Here's an energy-efficient technology if ever there was one. The now rather old-fashioned phone that simply plugs into the phone socket draws a mere fraction of a watt. The vast global telephone network is already built; and whilst it uses power and needs maintenance, its environmental footprint is hardly affected by your old-school phone calls.

Dark green:
No phone

For once, Luddism is not the greenest option. Unless you are the very grumpiest eco-hermit imaginable, you are going to want to communicate over distance. In the absence of a viable, sustainable carrier-pigeon network, this is going to mean lots of travelling. And this will have an impact even if it is human-powered, on account of all those extra calories you will need to make all the unnecessary journeys.

Quite green:
IP telephony over your computer

If you have a computer and Internet connection, using them for phone calls scores green points because you are making extra use of two existing resources and not plugging in new power-guzzling devices around the house. However, if your computer-based phoning means that the computer itself is switched on for longer, you might end up using more electricity, because even miserly laptops need at least five times as much power as a digital cordless base station. So this option is marginally greener only if you call whilst you are online anyway.

Light green:
Digital cordless phone

There are a couple of green issues with this technology. Firstly, the base station will draw about 5 watts, all the time, which is not much, but adds up to 43kWh per year. On a rough estimate of UK cordless-phone ownership, this amounts to over 700GWh per year, which is the output of 127 modern onshore wind turbines. The other issue is radiation. Official advice suggests that we have nothing to fear from the wireless network that every digital cordless telephone automati-cally creates in your house. But there are still plenty of people concerned about it, particularly those who consider themselves elec-tromagnetically sensitive.

Pale green:
Mobile phone

Whether the overall power demands of mobile-phone handsets exceed those of digital cordless phones is a tricky one. There are about three times as many mobile phones in circulation, but their chargers, which consume a couple of watts when doing their job, are not charging all the time. (However, they still draw a fraction of a watt when plugged in and switched on, and this all adds up too.) Mobile-phone networks, though, are pretty power-hungry, with 47,000 base stations currently needed to run their cellular networks in Britain. There is ongoing research into whether mobile-phone use can damage health; but a mast was recently removed in Britain following pressure from residents concerned about a cluster of cancers nearby. (Mobile-phone masts emit constant, low-level microwave radiation.) Mobile networks have even been fingered as a possible cause of 'colony collapse disorder' in honeybees.

Slightly paler green:
3G mobile phone

The base stations of this higher-bandwidth service have a lower radiation power output than standard GSM base stations. But because the width of a 3G cell is 8 kilometres as opposed to 35 kilometres for the standard network, many more masts will be needed, which means more power, infrastructure and radiation.

Television

*T*elevision: good or bad? If ever there was a question to stimulate cultural and environmental debate, this is one. The antis accuse telly of a corrosive effect on communities, family life, mental and physical health; they point to the energy guzzled by the average 2.4 TVs in every home, which accounts for over 6 per cent of total domestic electricity consumption and is rising fast because of digital TV and the over-use of 'standby'. And they remind us of the toxic environmental consequences when tellies are inevitably chucked away. In the opposite corner, TV fans point to educational, cultural and social benefits. And then there's the really difficult question: what would the 98 per cent of us who own TVs do with the 3.5 hours a day we spend (on average) watching them? Sit around knitting our own yoghurt in a yurt – or drive to the multiplex in our 4x4? Perhaps the planet is happier for us to stay on the sofa where we can do less damage . . .

Deep green:
No TV

The 'idiot's lantern', as curmudgeons dub it, is of course entirely unnecessary. Junking the big screen, digibox and DVD player (in an environmentally responsible way, of course) could save up to 550kWh per year and 240kg of CO_2 emissions, if you've been a heavy user. The TV-free can then spend more time resurrecting the dying art of their choice: reading, conversation, exercise, political activism – or even better, supporting their local pub, where for the price of a pint you will almost inevitably be able to cast a sneaky glance at someone else's TV (assuming you care about football).

Dark green:
Watch it on your laptop

Using a laptop computer to watch TV not only makes serious energy-saving sense, it also gives you low-cost access to digital TV wizardry. Laptops use around 30W when switched on, about one third of the power of the most energy-efficient standard TVs. For about £50, it is now possible to buy digital TV widgets that simply plug into your TV aerial and the laptop's USB port: thereafter you can watch the full range of Freeview channels as well as recording programmes and still images on the hard drive. Even if the laptop is used for nothing else, in energy terms this is about the greenest way of watching TV; but if the computer's use is shared with other applications, it's greener still. Another fine example of high technology being part of the solution rather than the problem. You could in fact be watching *Top Gear* when the others think you're huddled away in the corner of the tipi doing some green blogging.

Quite green:
OLEDs and FEDs

They're not here yet, so they don't really count. But projections suggest that plasma and LCD screens will be superseded later this decade by these technologies (organic light-emitting diodes and field effect diodes), the power consumption of which barely creeps into double figures of watts – hugely less than even the most miserly contemporary tellies.

Light green:
Small, old CRT monitor, analogue TV only

The cathode ray tube TV bucks the trend for old technologies being less efficient. Drawing an average 100W (about a quarter as much as an average hungry plasma screen), CRT TVs remain, on the whole, the most energy-efficient real-world option after laptops. So as long as it's not too big (in which case it will be more power-hungry), hang on to your old TV: by the time it expires, more efficient technologies may be here. And if you haven't got digital or satellite, waiting until the analogue signal is turned off before you upgrade will save you the energy consump-tion of a decoder, which ranges from about 9W (digital) to 18W (satellite or cable). This might save over 300kg of CO_2 emissions, assuming you live in one of the last areas to be switched off (the analogue switch-off runs from 2008 to 2012), watch an average amount of TV, use the hung-riest decoder and leave it in standby mode when not watching. Such savings (equivalent to not driving 1,100 miles in a standard car) must of course be weighed against the prospect of life with only five channels. Perhaps knocking out a few car journeys would be easier. Anyone consid-ering buying a CRT new should bear in mind that to achieve a (more desirable) flat screen, these TVs use more energy; and they can contain several kilos of lead, making landfill an even more undesirable final destination for them.

Pale green:
LCD

It's perhaps a little contentious to put LCDs down here. After all, the small ones use little more power than a laptop and in general LCDs are a better new buy than CRTs. But LCD TVs tend to be larger and thus often end up guzzling more power than their cathode-ray cousins – around 150W for a 32-inch model. Up to 15 per cent of them are also rejected at the production stage, making their manufacture relatively wasteful. However, there are LCDs on the market that have earned the EU's 'Ecolabel' badge, meaning that their production, energy use and disposal are environmentally 'good' relative to other models. The Energy Saving Trust also awards its 'recommended' badge to the more frugal LCDs. Products with integrated digital receivers are worth looking out for, too.

Not even a little bit green:

Massive plasma beast, satellite box, DVD player, the works

The monster plasma TV is indeed the SUV of the TV world. It can't be anything but big: plasma TVs under 32 inches are not viable; and they gulp more power per square inch of screen than any other TV technology. If your living room is well insulated, then a generous-sized plasma screen will at least provide some useful heating from the 400W it is likely to consume, particularly if this is augmented by, say, a satellite adapter, DVD player and (for they can be particularly energy-hungry) a games console. There are, of course, many more efficient ways to heat your house. In their defence, plasma screens are relatively easy to recycle and contain gold, which makes doing so attractive. However, with 90 per cent of their environmental impact happening during use rather than manufacture or disposal, plasma TVs' thirst for power gives them the ecological wooden spoon.

MORE INFORMATION
List of relatively energy-efficient televisions from the Energy Saving Trust: www.est.org.uk

Toilets

*W*hilst the humble water closet saved the nation from a host of communicable diseases back in the nineteenth century, today it has morphed into a bit of an ecological disaster area. It's mainly about water use (see p. 276 for more on water). Toilets are the biggest single users of fresh household drinking water, accounting for 35 per cent of all the water we use at home, or over 50 litres per person per day. We each use twice the amount of fresh drinking water needed for a person's basic subsistence just in order to make our bodily wastes go away. When parts of the UK have less water available per person than Sudan, this is a bit silly. Sewage treatment is also an energy guzzler, with its annual power demands equalling a quarter of the output of a big coal-fired power station. And whilst sewage treatment has come a long way from the days when it was simply hurled out of first-floor windows, 300 million gallons of the raw or partially treated stuff still make it into the environment each year, which is far from ideal. Finally, human waste is an under-exploited resource. Only 52 per cent of sewage sludge ends up on farmland as fertilizer (the rest is landfilled or burned): yet all of our wastes could be used to make our gardens happier.

Deep green:
Composting toilets and reed beds, being 'human-waste-neutral'

Amazingly, it is possible for your household to add no net human waste to the millions of tonnes of sewage that have to be treated each year. If you have enough land, there is of course the zero-cost, no-

251

technology option employed by other members of the animal kingdom. But the more civilized approach is to turn shit into gold. Solid waste can be turned into a benign, excellent fertilizer which is ideal for spreading around fruit bushes. This amazing process happens, discreetly, in composting toilets, of which a surprisingly large range of low- to high-tech variants are available. In a chamber, which can be anything from a wheelie bin to a large 'continuous' composting system, your faeces gracefully mutate into compost thanks to bacterial magic over a period of around a year. This usually takes space, though – maybe in a basement or an outhouse – so it won't be ideal for your twentieth-floor flat. Whilst they can be simple and home-made, composting toilets can also be major infrastructure projects and are certainly not suitable for every household. And despite the fact that these systems can be odour-free and involve normal-looking toilets rather than a scary 'black hole', neither do they suit everyone's sensibilities. Liquids can also be used on the land (see below) or can be treated with a 'reed-bed' system, in which aerobic bacteria work to purify the effluent. These can become an attractive garden feature and a haven for wildlife, but ideally need a bit of space and a sloping garden.

Dark green:
Minimal flushing, plus taking advantage of 'liquid gold'

Happily you do not have to spend any money at all in order to 'go' greenly. Reducing your water use is simply a matter of only flushing when something solid is involved. This can get a bit niffy but could save 80 per cent of your flushing water and thus nearly 30 per cent of your household water. Bad smells can of course be averted by diverting the offending substance; and this has additional advantages.

Urine, unexpectedly, is the worst offender in sewage terms, because removing the huge amount of unwanted nitrogen and phosphates it would otherwise release into the ecosystem adds considerably to the energy cost of sewage treatment. So it's far better to take advantage of urine's fertility where it is wanted: the garden. Neat urine can be applied directly to the compost heap, where it is an excellent 'activator' for the composting process. During the gardening season, diluted urine can be applied directly to food crops: it is the not-so-dirty secret of many successful allotment plots. Tomatoes in particular thrive on it and no one need ever know you keep a watering can in the loo.

Quite green:
A few bits of technology instead of behaviour changes

Anointing the garden and avoiding the flush are not, respectively, suitable for either the garden-free or squeamish. But there are still things you can do to limit the environmental impact of your bogs. The easiest is to target water use, which is where the modern toilet wreaks most ecological havoc. There will surely come a day when we will look back with amazement on the fact that we once used an average of 9 litres of expensively purified drinking water to wash away a few ccs of pee. A cut-down plastic bottle or bespoke sturdy bag (Savaflush or Hippo, for example) in the cistern will save 1–3 litres per flush. Spend a few quid and you can 'retrofit' a variable-flush handle to your cistern, giving different flush levels depending on the magnitude of the job to be dealt with. Whilst the legal requirement for new toilets is 6 litres, if you are refurbishing a house there are toilets available that use as little as 4.5 litres per flush. And any dual-flush model will reduce your toilet's thirst.

Not even a little bit green:

Very old-school or very high-tech toilets combined, of course, with obsessive flushing

The very oldest toilets, sadly often the handsome Victorian ones with a proper chain, use up to 13 litres each time their mighty, violent flush is used, so the profligate use of one of these will soon have the sewage system working overtime. Alternatively, you could opt for environmental destruction of another kind. High-tech toilets of the sort popular in Japan maybe use only 6 litres per flush, but with heated seats, warm-water-jet personal cleaning, air-drying and up to 1.3kW power demands, they account for 5 per cent of Japanese household energy use and are surely the best way really to drop one on the planet.

MORE INFORMATION
Alternative sewage factsheets and information available from the Centre for Alternative Technology: www.cat.org.uk

Tomatoes

*T*he sustainable tomato is a tricky thing to track down. By far the most ecologically benign option is also the tastiest: the sun-ripened flavour explosion that is a tomato grown outdoors in its natural season. But such delights are hard to come by. It is virtually impossible to buy a British outdoor tomato, even in the height of summer, because nearly all UK commercial production is in heated glasshouses. Even imports from more tomato-friendly climates in the Mediterranean are likely to have been grown under plastic, in an artificial substrate instead of soil. Taken away from their preferred warm climate and grown in a heated glasshouse, tomatoes are big energy guzzlers, needing 10kWh of power (the equivalent of leaving a one-bar electric fire on for ten hours) for every kilo of produce. But in warmer climates the yields are lower and the 50 litres of water needed to produce each kilo of tomatoes becomes an issue in water-stressed areas. And bear in mind too that, whilst they generally taste better, 'vine-ripened' tomatoes give a lower yield per square metre than 'loose' ones. So finding a planet-friendly tomato is a vexed business.

Deep green:
Your own tomatoes

Unless you are fortunate enough to be wandering a Mediterranean market in midsummer, it is unlikely that any tomato will match your own home-grown crop for flavour. Tomatoes are very easy to grow, even in small spaces, and place no demands on the environment if you irrigate them with rainwater, grow them in your own compost and fertilize them with 'liquid gold' (see p. 252). The only problem with this is that your window of tomato-eating is rather small, probably stretching only from August to October. It can be extended a little with an unheated greenhouse, but relying on your own crop will mean tomato famine for much of the rest of the year, unless you have gone to the trouble of growing a large surplus and bottling it.

Dark green:
Outdoor-grown tomatoes

Basking in solar radiation, outdoor tomatoes use almost one tenth of the energy of those grown in heated glasshouses, so score many eco-points from a fossil-fuel point of view. Sadly (or maybe happily), though, buying outdoor tomatoes means being on holiday somewhere Mediterranean, where markets will sell interesting varieties with outstanding flavour. Outdoor tomatoes are very susceptible to diseases, in particular the fungal disease blight, which is more well known for devastating potato crops. In the British climate, which is not (currently) very tomato-friendly, the controllability of the glasshouse environment means it is very hard to make outdoor growing competitive; as a result, it has all but died out here.

Light green:
Mediterranean imports

This third placing for foreign imports may rightly produce howls of protest from British tomato growers (see p. 257). Spain, from whence the majority of our imported tomatoes come (190,000 tonnes per year versus 78,500 grown locally) is a subject of concern for heavy pesticide use; for growing in short-lived polytunnels instead of long-lived glasshouses; and for excessive water abstraction in water-stressed areas. There is, however, no escaping the simple geographical facts of latitude and the sunshine that tomatoes crave; so even taking into account the food miles – which are mostly by lorry – Mediterranean tomatoes result in the release of three times less CO_2 than their more northerly glasshouse equivalents. Choosing tomatoes from, say, France or Italy may provide a less 'intensively reared' product.

Pale green:
UK glasshouse tomatoes

Could glasshouse tomatoes be one of those crops where, counter-intuitively, high-tech is sometimes better, at least in environmental terms? It does indeed take a lot of energy to produce a tomato (and to build the glasshouses and their complex systems). But pesticide use has been almost eliminated in UK tomato production as growers seek to use biological controls, such as natural pest predators, to deal with pests and diseases. The glasshouse environment offers protection against airborne diseases such as blight; and its irrigation water, which might otherwise leach unwanted nutrients into the environment, can be recycled. Some glasshouses are sited next to factories and take advantage of their waste heat; others are using combined heat and power (CHP) systems to achieve more energy efficiency (see also p. 140) and channelling some CO_2 into the greenhouse atmosphere to promote growth.

Slightly paler green:
UK glasshouse organic tomatoes

It's unusual and a wee bit controversial to find organics so far down the rankings. But if the issue is energy, statistics suggest there is no contest: organic growing needs nearly twice the energy and 20 per cent more water. And with conventional growers reducing pesticide use and planning to phase it out completely within ten years, the energy needed to manufacture agrochemicals is becoming less of an issue in the world of tomatoes. As are pesticide residues, which were found in only 23 per cent of UK samples in a recent survey: still not ideal, but a great deal better than for many other crops. However – organic tomatoes are grown in soil, rather than hydroponically and in an artificial substrate like Rockwool (which is also used for loft insulation). Whilst hydroponics advocates might suggest that this has no impact on the nutritional value of the tomato (because precisely metered nutrients are delivered directly to the plant), intuition suggests that a better balance of minerals and nutrients might be derived from real soil whose fertility has been naturally enhanced.

Not even a little bit green:
Dutch glasshouse tomatoes

Holland is the next biggest exporter of tomatoes to the UK, trucking 90,000 tonnes to us each year – more than we produce ourselves. With a similar climate to Britain's, Holland has no energy advantage; add on the food miles and Dutch tomatoes lose out to our own in environmental terms.

Tomato season

UK glasshouse crops and Mediterranean
imports (UK crops heated in cooler months)

UK outdoor tomato season

| J | F | M | A | M | J | J | A | S | O | N | D |

Trains

Are trains the eco-friendly transport solution they are often cracked up to be? There is not a simple, straightforward answer; and any clarity on the subject is immediately muddied by the various lobbies involved – pro-aviation, pro-car, anti-car, trainspotters – all of whom are out to prove that theirs is the best and also the greenest way forward. Sometimes the trouble that people go to in order to work out environmental impacts is fascinating. A German scientist has gone to quite nerdy lengths to establish whether it would be greener to travel from Frankfurt to Kobe in Japan by plane or train. The answer is train, by a factor of two, or much more if an aircraft's estimated 'radiative forcing' effect (see p. 5) is taken into account. The journey takes a wee bit longer, though. Trains can offer better greenhouse-gas performance than planes or cars, although not always by the big margins you might expect. And once they start to go really fast (200+ k.p.h.), trains' power consumption rapidly eats into their environmental advantage.

Deep green:
Get there under your own steam

There is no such thing as an eco-friendly train. Electric trains may be emission-free (at least from the train itself), but with multiple 280kW motors they're sucking down plenty of juice, which is produced in power stations at less than 40 per cent efficiency and generated, in this country, mainly by fossil fuels. In general, it is even greener to take a coach, which on the whole offers better emissions per passenger kilometre, but the true hardcore greenie will eschew such comforts and get pedalling. With practice, covering 200 kilometres in a day by bicycle becomes no big deal, is entirely carbon-neutral and means you don't have to listen to all those annoying mobile-phone conversations.

Dark green:
Crammed on to a local commuter train

Much as we might lament the lost branch lines of old, it's a straight fact of physics that a 40-ton train with a 300-horsepower engine and three people on board is going to do what the Americans call 'lousy gas mileage' per passenger. It will kick out nearly 500 grams of CO_2 per kilometre for each passenger, almost twice the per-occupant emissions of a Bugatti Veyron (see p. 59). Fill a train to capacity, though, and it's a different matter entirely. The same train, full to bursting with commuters, is now doing only 18 grams per kilometre per passenger, which is better than can be achieved on a coach and far, far better than going by car. Trains are at their greenest when they are on high-demand lines and not going too fast. So when you are packed on to a standing-room-only train, struggling to read the paper amongst a babble of inane "I'm on the train!"-type conversations, it may come as some small crumb of comfort to know that you are doing your bit for the environment.

Pale green:
High-speed train (in France)

It feels terribly virtuous to take the Eurostar to Paris rather than devastating the environment with a short-haul flight (see p. 5). But are such 300 k.p.h. trains better for the planet than a small airliner? Push trains past 200 k.p.h. and the power they need increases massively. High-speed trains like the Eurostar have power outputs of 6,000+kW – equivalent to about a hundred cars. Research suggests that over long journeys high-speed trains are no greener in terms of energy consumption than planes. However, this doesn't take into account all the environmental 'externalities' of travel, such as impacts on nature, climate change and noise: on these, the impact of air transport is calculated to be significantly worse. Go to France for your high-speed train experience, though, and it's greener still, at least in terms of CO_2 emissions, because French TGV trains are electric, and in France nearly 80 per cent of electricity is generated by nuclear power. Now nukes, of course, have one or two environmental issues of their own, and neither the vast energy needed to extract and enrich uranium nor the fact that, like oil, it is a finite resource is talked about much by nuclear energy's promoters. But it's still a relatively low-CO_2 way of generating power and, seeing as the infrastructure is all there, France currently offers the best way to travel at very high speeds for low emissions.

Not even a little bit green:
Cute old steam engine

Admittedly there are very few cute old steam engines knocking about in the UK these days and their relative contribution to our environmental ills is pretty minimal. Steam trains could in theory be run on biofuels, as could diesel-engined trains; and whilst this would have some environmental benefits (see p. 56 for the issues surrounding biofuels), a coal tender sloshing about with waste cooking oil would immediately remove much of the romance from a steam engine. In general, steam engines are less efficient, need copious supplies of water as well as fuel and kick out nasty emissions directly into areas of high population. Given the emotions stirred by steam, it will come as no surprise to learn that enthusiasts are working on a new-generation steam locomotive designed to run on multiple fuels and be much more efficient than previous models. But with steam locomotives labour-intensive to operate as well as ecologically noxious, it seems unlikely that they will make a comeback in an era that is concerned with cost-cutting as well as carbon.

MORE INFORMATION
A detailed analysis of the relative ecological merits of getting from Frankfurt to Kobe by train or plane:
http://www.sgr.org.uk/kyoto/ecobal.html

Turkey

You'd think that turkey would have only a once-yearly impact on the environment. But of the 17 million turkeys produced for meat in the UK in a year, fewer than half are consumed at Christmas: the rest can be found throughout the food chain, from cooked meat to ready meals to hot dogs. Because of its relatively small scale, turkey production is unlikely to bring about ecological apocalypse single-handedly (unless via avian influenza); fifty times as many chickens are raised for meat every year (see p. 60) in an industry that consumes a great deal more in the way of natural resources. In total, poultry is the single biggest consumer of wheat, gobbling 20 per cent of the UK harvest.

Dark green:
Slow-growing organic turkey, just for Christmas

After applying the usual caveat to carnivores that the greenest diet of all is meat-free (see also p. 164), the best turkeys for your tastebuds and the planet are slow-growing breeds raised outdoors on a small scale, organically. These will not need energy-intensive growing operations; and whilst the few fine upstanding turkeys raised by the local farmer may not be certified organic, those that are will be eating feed that was less energy-intensive to produce. So if we're being picky, organic is a slightly better eco-bet even if the local farmer's birds may have been reared in similar welfare conditions and taste just as good. Breeds to look out for are the Norfolk (Kelly) Bronze and the Norfolk Black, which can spend up to six months flapping around and flexing their muscles before facing their appointment with festive destiny. Limiting your turkey consumption to the annual Christmas feast wins on two scores: clearly it's a good form of meat reduction; also, because many small producers raise birds specifically for the Christmas market, your choice of well-reared birds will be much greater than at other times of year.

Not particularly green:
Cheap turkey for Christmas

Figures for the chicken industry suggest that intensive rearing in packed sheds is over 30 per cent more energy-efficient than 'extensive' free-range systems, mainly because the intensive chickens live only half as long and thus consume much less food. Comparative figures do not exist for the turkey industry, but the age gap is the same, with birds reared intensively indoors being slaughtered at as little as three months. The sheds may use a little more energy (turkeys like to be warm) but less light, because dimness tempers their considerable capacity for aggression. So it could well be that in energy terms industrial turkey is greener. But if you factor animal welfare into the green calculation, it loses out: the over-bred birds which put on weight at a startling rate are prone to leg injuries and need to be assisted in mating, a process which is profoundly undignified for both turkey and handler. Add nutritional and gourmet value into the equation and the bland meat of an intensive turkey is streets behind its gamier, more flavoursome outdoor counterpart.

Not even a little bit green:
Processed turkey

Buy processed turkey and it will almost certainly have been intensively reared before having 'value' added to it with the inclusion of all
manner of additives: water, milk proteins, sweeteners, starch, flavourings and more. The production of all these carries an environmental
cost, as does the enticing packaging involved. The only party getting
'value' out of intensive processed turkey is the producer.

Washing and drying clothes

*O*nly those with the very hairiest of hair shirts would consider giving up a washing machine to save the planet. But would it be the right thing to do anyway? Hand-washing is neither particularly efficient nor much fun, even if you have a mangle. Like dishwashers, although not to the same degree, washing machines are another example of technology using resources efficiently. The fact remains, though, that washing and drying clothes uses about 12 per cent of the 150 litres of water an average person uses every day; and up to 10 per cent of our annual electricity consumption. There are ways of managing this down; and, as always, there are some extreme options too.

Deep green:
Minimal, biofuel-heated hand-washing in harvested rainwater

The price you pay for ultra-greenness in the world of washing is sheer hard work and/or being a bit whiffy. Washing clothes affects the environment mainly through the use of fresh water and the energy needed to heat it; and to a lesser degree through the impact of the waste water. If you are really serious about sustainable washing, then you can deal completely with all of these. Using harvested rainwater (see also below) means that valuable drinking water is not wasted. Biofuels mean the water is heated carbon-neutrally. And hand-washing needs no electricity and confers the added benefit of a

267

reasonable upper-body workout. But seeing as a single fill of a butler sink will use as much water as a typical washing machine cycle (50 litres), too much hand-washing will quickly exhaust your water supplies. So the washes should be few and far between, requiring what someone in a marketing meeting might term 'a recalibration in personal odour tolerance levels'. Natural soaps rather than perfumed detergents will eliminate pollution from the waste water, which in such a pristine state could even go on the veg patch to complete the virtuous hydrological cycle. And it goes without saying that clothes-drying should be free of any technology or fossil fuels. Recondition that Victorian mangle!

Dark green:
Communal laundering

It is a hard fact of greenness that the best thing to do is often to do things together. Sharing things that have a major environmental impact – a house, a car, bulk food delivery – is often the biggest single thing you can do to reduce your 'footprint'. A study cited by the Women's Environmental Network showed that laundry services for washable nappies – in which the offending items are taken away, dealt with and returned – used 32 per cent less energy than home washing and 41 per cent less water. So whether it's a posh concierge-style laundry service, a team trip to the launderette or the communal laundry of a co-housing project, the chances are that sharing the load is going to be greener than having your own machines. However, it is not necessarily going to be more convenient or cheaper.

Quite green:

A + or AA-rated appliances, used sparingly at low temperatures (with optional harvested rainwater for ultra-greenie points), minimal detergent use and 'natural' drying

All washing machines have a rating for energy consumption, washing and spin-drying performance and the mandatory energy label on new machines tells you how they score. (There's a link to an eco-ranking of machines below.) A 40°C wash uses almost half the energy of a 60°C wash (about 0.6kWh per cycle on an A-rated machine), so dropping the wash temperature is an easy, immediate way to reduce a machine's energy use. Old machines will use significantly more energy and water, so it is worth replacing them. And yes, it can be green to buy a new one, because around 90 per cent of a washing machine's environmental impact is in its use, versus only 10 per cent in its manufacture and disposal. For extra green points you could eliminate mains water use in your washing machine altogether with a rainwater-harvesting system. For a couple of thousand pounds, such a system can also feed your toilets (the biggest water users in a household; see p. 251) as well as the washing machine, baths, showers, laundry and garden. As for your choice of detergent, phosphate-free brands are worth seeking out: although on the decline, phosphates from clothes- and dish-washing are still implicated in the eutrophication (over-enrichment) of ecosystems and water companies have to remove them in a complex chemical process. That said, eco-friendly brands are not without their problems, so minimizing detergent use is always the best bet. As for drying, there's still no such thing as a green tumble dryer, despite the existence of gas-powered models (much better for CO_2 emissions) and low-energy models using heat-pump technology that manage a 'mere' 2.1kWh per cycle. So it's the washing line in the warm months – and in the winter, there's little to beat a Victorian-style drying rack (of which modern exemplars are available for much less cost than a tumble dryer).

Not even a little bit green:
Frequent washes, over-zealous use of a C-rated tumble dryer, nasty detergents

As with so many things, it's simplicity itself to wreak havoc on the environment with washing. Do a couple of washes a day (at 60°C, naturally) and you'll soon be using nearly 40,000 litres of drinking water a year. Whilst this will also use a fair amount of electricity, bringing the tumble dryer into play for each wash will really crank it up. Given that there exist 'upscale' communities where hanging out the washing is frowned upon, let's assume the dryer gets used for each wash, every day of the year: do this and you could almost achieve the average UK energy consumption from washing and drying alone. And really to kick the planet when it's down, use old-school detergents and unnecessary fabric conditioners and softeners to release pollutants and unnecessary packaging into the environment.

Not even a little bit green 2:
Dry cleaning

Here's a simple test to see whether you think dry cleaning is green. Would you do it in your own house? As the smell fills the utility room, the idea of washing your clothes in solvents might lose any appeal it had. The industry may say that the principal chemical used in dry cleaning (perchloroethylene or 'perc') is safe, but plenty of others (including the US Environmental Protection Agency) suggest it may have health implications, pointing out that among other things it is a toxic pollutant that adversely affects the central nervous system. Truly green alternatives don't really exist, although silicon-based 'GreenEarth', being introduced by some UK firms, is less bad than perc, and there's a CO_2-based process being introduced (but let's hope they capture and store the emissions). Buying fewer dry-clean-only clothes (or ignoring the instruction) is the best bet.

MORE INFORMATION

Green ranking of washing machines: www.waterwise.org

Washing dishes

Taken to extremes, a measure of the greenness or otherwise of washing up could be extended to weigh up, say, the bonhomie of a gung-ho family dish-wash versus the cold solitary hum of the dishwasher. Most of us, however, are interested in just one simple question: is it better for the environment to do it by hand or not? For once, there's an answer here to cheer the majority of us who hate washing up yet love the planet.

Deep green:
Using leaves, eating exclusively at an old-fashioned chippy, or washing the dishes with filtered rainwater

OK, so these are either silly or very complicated. But they serve to illustrate that it's hard to get greener than the next greenest option, which is, surprisingly, to use a modern dishwasher. Even the most fastidious washers-up will use more water and energy per item of crockery or cutlery than one of these. So you need to visit the wilder shores of greenness to beat one. Perhaps you could find a source of banana leaves, which make excellent plates, don't need washing and are fully compostable. Or maybe you could eat exclusively at your local, traditional chip shop, thus boosting local business and creating only biodegradable waste (although the greasy newspaper will have to be burnt, because it won't compost happily). Doing the dishes with filtered rainwater from your roof gets round the water-usage issues, but putting in the necessary gubbins to store and distribute rainwater, and filter it to drinking-water standards, is a major undertaking.

Dark green:
AAA-rated dishwasher, used only when full

Hardcore environmentalists may harrumph that a product of evil consumerist society couldn't possibly be the best option. But it's hard to argue against the dishwasher. With the latest models using 15 litres per cycle or less, mechanical dishwashing uses only a quarter of the water needed by an average hands-on session at the sink. Over a ten-year lifespan, a dishwasher could save a British household 100,000 litres. So scale up national household dishwasher usage from the current 30-odd per cent and you have a recipe for serious water-saving. And even if you account for the relative inefficiency of a dishwasher's electrical water-heating, at around 1kWh per cycle it uses less energy than old-school washing-up too. You can even mitigate this issue by going against the manufacturer's recommendations and plumbing it into the hot-water supply. However, there are a couple of caveats with dishwashers. They only stay green if run when full: firing them up for just a few plates soon knocks out the green benefits and the 'half load' settings typically use more than half the power and water of a full cycle. And some dishwasher detergents contain a powerful hit of chlorine – not a pleasant substance – and phosphates, which cause problems if their residues make it into watercourses. So choosing eco-friendly detergents – and using them sparingly – helps to keep the dishwasher extra green. Look for appliances rated AAA (for energy consumption, cleaning and drying performance respectively), and check out dishwasher league tables (see p. 274).

Quite green:
Incredibly fastidious manual dishwashing, re-using the greywater.

Despite the estimate that 90 per cent of a dishwasher's environmental impact is in its use and only 10 per cent in its production and disposal, there may still be some who cannot quite square green with technology, especially when it's as much fun as a dishwasher. And of course there are those not fortunate enough to be able to afford one; and also 'off-gridders' (see p. 111) who want to save their meagre electricity reserves for really important applications, like listening to music. For the dishwasher-free, green washing-up means either the daft deep-green options above or being very careful at the sink. This entails rinsing in a separate bowl rather than under a running tap and the use of eco-friendly detergent so that the carefully saved waste water won't upset the plants, on to which it is to be chucked. Even with all these measures it will be a stretch to keep the water consumption down to the 15 (or even 10) litres that the best dishwashers can manage.

Pale green:
Manky old dishwasher, still hanging in there

Even if your dishwasher dates from the 1970s, which is unlikely, it will still use less water to wash a full load than an average British washing-up session (around 50 litres vs 63). And getting the maximum use out of an appliance is always a good idea, unless it is a complete energy vampire. That said, if you can afford to replace such a machine, a £200 contemporary model could eventually pay for itself if you are on a metered water supply.

Not even a little bit green:
Doing it the old-fashioned way

Washing the dishes is one of those rare parts of modern life where progress, happily, does not equal ecological devastation. The old way is definitely not the best. To achieve the same effect as a dishwasher you will need plenty of piping hot water (electrically heated for maximum 'ecocide' points) and of course a constantly running hot water tap to get a good clean rinse. Do all this after a big meal and you could be using 150 litres of water and four times the energy a modern dishwasher needs to achieve the same effect. Gaia wants you to stop washing up by hand. Great, isn't it?

MORE INFORMATION
Efficient dishwashers listed at the
Energy Saving Trust website: www.est.org.uk
Also at www.waterwise.org.uk

Water (supply)

The provision of clean drinking water and sewage services beat antibiotics, vaccines and anaesthesia to be voted the greatest medical milestone of the last century and a half in a British Medical Journal poll. Today, all of us have a precious resource piped into our homes courtesy of much technology, infrastructure and expense. We then proceed to waste well over 50 per cent of it on jobs for which purified drinking water is completely unnecessary (and arguably inferior in some cases): washing clothes, watering the garden and, daftest of all, flushing away our bodily wastes. Our water use has tripled over the last hundred years (rising by 70 per cent in the last twenty years alone) to an average of 150 litres per person per day thanks to our fondness for second bathrooms, power showers and excessive personal hygiene. The amount of water needed to sustain our basic needs varies between 20 and 80 litres per day, depending on what counts as a basic need. Should you care about all this? It's hard to bother if you live, say, in the Lake District, Snowdonia or western Scotland, which get more than twice the UK average annual rainfall. However, elsewhere in the country there are varying degrees of water stress and shortage; and water bills are expected to keep rising in coming years as companies work to meet our demands and strict environmental regulations. So green water behaviour can make economic as well as ecological sense.

Deep green:
Water neutrality

This means taking nothing from the public water supply and putting nothing back into the public sewage network, thus relieving stress on the environment and the water companies and giving you 'water autonomy' to boot. You can achieve water neutrality the simple-but-tough way: living rough in the woods, drinking from streams and doing what bears do; or you can do it the complex and more agreeable way, by building your own water supply and sewage systems. The best way to get the water is through rainwater harvesting (see below). Depending on where you live, this could potentially supply all your water needs, especially when combined with greywater recycling, a potentially more complex and smelly business. Solid wastes can be dealt with using dry composting toilets (see p. 251) and liquids by using a reed-bed system. Next time someone wrinkles their nose near a sewage farm, you will be able to say 'It wasn't me!'

Dark green:
Rainwater harvesting and water-saving measures

Being water-neutral is a potentially expensive and high-tech business. You'll need a big storage tank to tide you over rain-free periods and the rainwater you plan to drink will need additional UV purification. All this needs investment and, of course, it uses power too (see drinking water, p. 96). Marginally easier is just harvesting rainwater to flush your toilets, wash your clothes and water the garden, which together account for 54 per cent of household water use. Even the roof of a small terraced house in the semi-arid south-east of England could capture 30,000 litres per year, which is useful, if nowhere near enough to slake the water-thirst of a family with a 150-litres-per-person-per-day habit. Systems cost upwards of £2,000 installed (and you'll still need the big tank and the power) and payback times currently run into decades, but rising water costs are likely to bring an earlier return on investment. There is not really any point in doing serious rainwater harvesting unless you are going for serious water-saving measures (see below) at the same time. But there is also a school of thought that suggests simple, cheap water-saving measures are potentially greener than high-tech water harvesting and recycling, because they need no power and minimal infrastructure.

Dark green 2:

Lots of water-saving measures, a water meter, a water butt or two for the garden

Water-saving measures fall into two categories: those that involve behaviour change and those that use technology. The former are easy, but not to everyone's taste. Less flushing of the toilet, which is the biggest single (and most illogical) household water consumer, is the most effective thing to do, but the 'if it's yellow, let it mellow' rule does have an olfactory downside. Other examples of behaviour changes are showers (35 litres) instead of baths (80 litres), minimal car-washing, no watering the garden. A bit of technology can also make a difference: cheap (or free) cistern displacement devices like Hippo bags will save 3 litres per flush; spray taps can use 80 per cent less water; and the most efficient dishwashers and washing machines (see pp. 269 and 273) are becoming quite miserly and, thankfully, are more water-efficient than doing the tasks by hand. Add in a water meter, which is proven to reduce demand by making you more conscious of your use, and a cheap water butt or two to take care of the garden, and watery dark-greenness can be yours for minimal outlay and could start saving you money immediately.

Quite green:
Just having a meter

Imagine un-metered energy. Would we use less? As if. Our houses would be lit up like Christmas trees, kept at subtropical temperatures in winter and air-conditioned in summer. So until you get a meter, only environmental conscience is stopping you from going wild with the water. Stick one in, however, and it turns into a numbers game. Water profligacy will soon mean you pay more than before, so on average, households cut their usage by about 10 per cent once a meter is installed. But cutting more presents the possibility of real financial savings: nothing to get too excited about, as the water portion of the average annual water and sewerage bill is currently only £134 per year, but it's a saving that will increase as prices inevitably rise.

Not even a little bit green:
No meter, no water-saving, pool, jacuzzi, power shower, constant car-washing – the whole (water) works

This is the expensive route to water profligacy: you could of course just leave the tap running or have leaks everywhere. But for really effective reservoir depletion coupled with maximum collateral environmental damage (through heating, chemicals and materials costs), pools, hot tubs and jacuzzis can use tens of thousands of litres over the year, cranking your household water use up to a level that could provide a subsistence supply for the population of a small hamlet.

MORE INFORMATION
Guides and factsheets available from:
Centre for Alternative Technology: www.cat.org.uk
Environment Agency: www.environment-agency.gov.uk
Waterwise: www.waterwise.org.uk

Wine

Stormtroopers of the environmental movement might be moved to condemn wine, together with other alcoholic drinks (see also p. 38), as entirely unnecessary to human survival and therefore a waste of land, energy and resources. One imagines, however, that such stormtroopers are thin on the ground. Anyway, it has been suggested that getting mildly 'out of it' is part of the human condition; and it's certainly better for the planet if we employ a decent Sauvignon Blanc rather than a few lines of cocaine (see p. 100) to achieve the desired effect. A 'life cycle analysis' of wine production shows that the most significant ways in which it affects the environment are through the agricultural activities needed to make it and the production of the bottles in which it is almost always packaged. As to whether it's a terrible thing to buy wine from very far away – the issue is not as clear as it is often presented. Some Antipodean producers are adopting standards which are aimed at countering the environmental costs of long-distance shipping.

Deep green:
Make your own

Winemaking is a low-impact process, involving relatively little in the way of energy and resources. Make your own and you can be in total control of the evening tipple's ecological footprint. Those surplus parsnips from the allotment that no one can face eating? Turn them into wine. Overgrown marrows? Wine. There are no wine miles and you can keep re-using the bottles: this has to be the most cost-effective, eco-friendly way of achieving intoxication (apart, of course, from the more extreme and now highly illegal route of foraging for hallucinogenic mushrooms, see p. 100).

Dark green:
Live in a wine-producing region and buy it wholesale

Although winemaking could well creep further north up the UK as the climate warms, this option is currently easier if you move to a more southerly country. (There is an extra ecological argument for doing this, inasmuch as your heating bills could be lower too.) Filling up an enormous container at the winemaker's and bottling it by hand at home (in re-used bottles, of course) will give you a supply of wine that will be good for a year, cost a great deal less than the bottled version and result in the expenditure of much less packaging and transport energy.

Quite green:
Local and organic

This is a difficult call for the British. We have become accustomed to the big shouty flavours of wines from sunny places and are suspicious of the output of our own industry, which none the less produces some very respectable wines. Whilst wine miles (see p. 283) may not be anything like as big an issue as they are for produce that is routinely air-freighted, buying locally does minimize the impact of transportation. And buying organic encourages sustainable winemaking. Conventional wine uses doses of pesticides, fungicides and herbicides that are said to be most heavily applied in the highest-yielding wine-growing areas of France and Australia. This is not so much of an issue from a health point of view, because the fermentation process takes care of any residues; however, as with other forms of agriculture, it has an impact on soil health and biodiversity as well as involving energy-intensive industrial products. Lower levels of sulphur are used in the organic process, which it is claimed make for less severe hangovers.

Light green:
Biodynamic, from anywhere

Biodynamic agriculture, in essence, is organic with knobs on. It takes the organic process a stage further, attending not only to the health of the soil but seeing the farm as an ecological system and the soil as an organism. Based on the philosophy of Rudolf Steiner, the wackier elements of whose philosophy lead some biodynamic producers to distance themselves from him, it involves, among other things, working with lunar cycles and using strange preparations to bring life to the soil. Despite all this spookiness, biodynamic practice is catching on amongst wine producers, for the simple reason that it produces great wine. Because it is also great for the environment, biodynamic wine is a good eco-choice whether it was grown in the UK or has sailed halfway round the world.

Pale green:
'Certified' wines from anywhere

Most wine is shipped, which produces around a hundred times less CO_2 per tonne/kilometre than air freight. (A notable exception is the time-critical Beaujolais Nouveau, whose air-freighting to Tokyo alone is responsible for over 6,000 tonnes of CO_2 emissions). Still, there's no getting away from the fact that shipping heavy stuff halfway round the world carries an ecological cost. But as with other shipped products (see also lamb, p. 152), it's not a simple case of 'imports bad, local good'. Biodynamic wine from thousands of miles away, for example, may compare favourably in eco-footprint terms with wine produced in Europe by intensive, agrochemical-heavy means. Some countries and producers are getting wise to this issue. New Zealand producers have the option to brand themselves 'CarboNZero', which aims to offset the impact of shipping with good environmental practice elsewhere. Fairtrade wines will have been produced with a focus on environmental preservation as well as workers' rights. And by 2009, all exported South African wines will have a certification that ensures they are produced with biodiversity and the environment in mind.

Not even a little bit green:
Intensively produced wine from far away

Wine from big, industrial-scale operations is most likely to have been produced with energy-intensive pesticides, herbicides and fungicides. And whilst shipping may not be the biggest component of your tipple's carbon footprint, buying such wine from the furthest possible destination will ensure the footprint is as big as possible. Of course, if you really want to use wine as the centrepiece of an eco-destruction strategy, flying to Tokyo (in a private jet, of course) to drink Beaujolais Nouveau would do the trick.